Women in Alternative Finance

Francesca Battaglia · Emanuela Giusi Gaeta

Women in Alternative Finance

Exploring the Benefits of Equity Crowdfunding

palgrave
macmillan

Francesca Battaglia
Associate Professor of Banking and Finance
University of Naples Parthenoepe
Naples, Italy

Emanuela Giusi Gaeta
Economic and Financial Analyst for the Italian Treasury Department
Rome, Italy

Francesca Battaglia (Corresponding author) conceived and designed the entire book, wrote Chapters 1, 4 and 5, and is the coauthor of Chapter 3
Emanuela Giusi Gaeta wrote Chapter 2 and is coauthor of Chapter 3.

ISBN 978-3-031-43466-2 ISBN 978-3-031-43467-9 (eBook)
https://doi.org/10.1007/978-3-031-43467-9

This Palgrave Macmillan imprint is published by the registered company Springer Nature Switzerland AG
The registered company address is: Gewerbestrasse 11, 6330 Cham, Switzerland

Paper in this product is recyclable.

Contents

About the Authors

Francesca Battaglia is Associate Professor of Banking and Finance in the Department of Business Economics and Quantitative Methods, at the University of Naples Parthenoepe. She obtained her PhD from the University of Rome Tor Vergata. She holds several external academic positions, including as Visiting Scientist at the Joint Research Centre (JRC) of the European Commission in the field of sustainable finance. Moreover, she is Academic Fellow at the Centre for Responsible Banking and Finance of the University of St Andrews. She is Associate Editor of the *International Journal of Finance and Economics, the Corporate Governance* (*The International Journal of Business in Society*), the *Global Business Review*, and *Helyion.*

Her research interests include risk management and performance of financial intermediaries, securitisation, corporate governance, fintech, carbon finance, and sustainability performance. Francesca has published in several journals, including the *European Journal of Finance*, the *Journal of International Financial Markets, Institutions and Money, Research in International Business and Finance*, and the *International Review of Financial Analysis.*

Emanuela Giusi Gaeta received a PhD in Political Economy at Sapienza University; she was Researcher in Political Economy at Tor Vergata University and Supervisor of Research Projects in Criminal Economy.

She teaches courses on Political Economy, Political Economics, Monetary Economics, International Economics, Applied Economics, Criminal Economy, and Endogenous Growth course at the Research Doctorate. She actually works as Economic and Financial Analyst for the Italian Treasury Department.

Her research areas are Cryptocurrencies Market, Energy-Saving Technologies, Technological Transfer, and Criminal Economy.

List of Figures

List of Tables

CHAPTER 1

Introduction

Francesca Battaglia

Abstract This chapter introduces the topics that will be covered in the following chapters of the book, by showing the reasons that led us to address this topic. As in the existing literature, there is substantial evidence that women are penalised with respect to men in many funding markets (i.e. private equity, institutional capital, and bank financing), female entrepreneurs have to find an answer elsewhere and seek funding from alternative channels. With this regard, there is some early evidence that women are not at a disadvantage compared to men in crowdfunding, where they even seem to perform better.

Keywords Female entrepreneurship · Alternative funding channels · Crowdfunding · Female-led successful campaigns · Crowdfunding regulation

The existing body of literature provides substantial evidence that women are penalised compared to men in many funding markets. This includes private equity (e.g. Becker-Blease and Sohl 2007), institutional capital (e.g. Bigelow et al. 2014b), and bank financing (e.g. Eddleston et al. 2016; Ongena and Popov 2015; Alesina et al. 2013; Hertz 2011; Muravyev et al. 2009; Fay and Williams 1993; Buttner and Rosen 1988). This makes the weight of female entrepreneurship strictly minority in

F. Battaglia and E. Giusi Gaeta, *Women in Alternative Finance*,
https://doi.org/10.1007/978-3-031-43467-9_1

some fields, as demonstrated by Canning et al. (2012), who found that female-led firms obtain a mere 1.3% of venture capital financing. According to a survey conducted by Bloomberg, which examined 890 start-ups in the United States during the year 2016, it was determined that a mere 7% of the founders were women. Furthermore, the report indicates that these female entrepreneurs received much less funding compared to their male counterparts. Based on data provided by PitchBook and All Raise, prominent organisations advocating for women in the venture capital and start-up sectors, *Fortune* (https://fortune.com/2019/01/28/funding-female-founders-2018/) reveals that female founders in the United States secured a total of $2.88 billion in funding during 2018. This amount represents a mere 2.2% of the overall $130 billion invested in venture capital throughout the year. It is noteworthy that this percentage remains consistent with the figures reported for the preceding year, 2017 (the exact same percentage was reported for 2017).

Data provided by the European Commission (https://ec.europa.eu/growth/smes/promoting-entrepreneurship/we-work-for/women_en) supports the findings observed in the United States, indicating that women who embark on entrepreneurship encounter various obstacles. These challenges include limited access to financial resources, information, business networks, and training. Additionally, women entrepreneurs often face difficulties in balancing their business responsibilities with familial obligations. In order to address this predicament, the European Commission is actively engaged in efforts to foster more female participation in entrepreneurial endeavours. This is being accomplished through the implementation of the Small Business Act and the Entrepreneurship 2020 Action Plan, which serve to promote and provide assistance for women in their pursuit of establishing their own businesses.

Lacking access to conventional venture capital, female entrepreneurs are compelled to explore alternate avenues and secure money from sources outside the usual realm, such as crowdfunding platforms. There is some early evidence that women do not have a disadvantage relative to males in the context of crowdfunding, and in fact, they appear to exhibit superior performance (e.g. Zhao et al. 2020; Johnson et al. 2018; Mollick and Robb 2016). The 2017 PwC report "Women Unbound: Unleashing female entrepreneurial potential" based on 2015 and 2016 seed crowdfunding data shows that—even though men raise more finance than women—crowdfunding female-led campaigns significantly outperform those led by men in terms of probability of success. The analysis covers about 465,000 seed crowdfunding campaigns from nine of the largest global crowdfunding platforms showing that female-led campaigns were 32% more successful at reaching their funding target than male-led campaigns. Even in sectors that are traditionally perceived as being dominated by males, such as the technology industry, where the ratio of male-led campaigns to female-led efforts is nine to one, it has been observed that female-led ads have achieved a higher level of success, with a success rate of 13% compared to 10% for male-led initiatives. Furthermore, it is worth noting that in both the United States and the United Kingdom, which are recognised as the countries with the highest campaign volumes, the success rates of male-led campaigns were observed to be 20%, while the success rates of female-led campaigns were somewhat higher at 24% and 26%, respectively.

The primary objective of this book is to present fresh empirical findings on the relationship between female entrepreneurship and alternative financing, with a specific emphasis on the realm of equity crowdfunding. The main idea underlying this research is that while women generally find disadvantage with respect to male counterparts in traditional credit markets, this seems not to be the case for alternative funding channels like crowdfunding, as empirical evidence shows.

The distinctive aspect of the book is the focus on the equity crowdfunding market which could be considered as the perfect ground to develop and to grow up the female entrepreneurial skills; from this point of view, the book gives a clear recommendation to policymakers about how to support women in alternative finance, by providing more specific and detailed rules and action plans focusing on this topic.

References

Alesina, A. F., Lotti, F., and Mistrulli, P. E. (2013). Do women pay more for credit? Evidence from Italy. *Journal of the European Economic Association*, *11*(suppl_1), 45–66.

Becker-Blease, J. R., and Sohl, J. E. (2007). Do women-owned businesses have equal access to angel capital? *Journal of Business Venturing*, *22*(4), 503–521.

Bigelow, C. A., Pereira, G. A., Warmsley, A., Cohen, J., Getrajdman, C., Moshier, E., and Stone, J. (2014a). Risk factors for new-onset late postpartum preeclampsia in women without a history of preeclampsia. *American Journal of Obstetrics and Gynecology*, *210*(4), 338-e1.

Bigelow, L., Lundmark, L., McLean Parks, J., and Wuebker, R. (2014b). Skirting the issues: Experimental evidence of gender bias in IPO prospectus evaluations. *Journal of Management*, *40*(6), 1732–1759.

Buttner, E. H., and Rosen, B. (1988). Bank loan officers' perceptions of the characteristics of men, women, and successful entrepreneurs. *Journal of Business Venturing*, *3*(3), 249–258.

Canning, J., Haque, M., and Wang, Y. (2012). *Women at the wheel: Do female executives drive start-up success*. Dow Jones and Company.

Eddleston, K. A., Ladge, J. J., Mitteness, C., and Balachandra, L. (2016). Do you see what I see? Signaling effects of gender and firm characteristics on financing entrepreneurial ventures. *Entrepreneurship Theory and Practice*, *40*(3), 489–514.

Fay, M., and Williams, L. (1993). Gender bias and the availability of business loans. *Journal of Business Venturing*, *8*(4), 363–376.

Hertz, N. (2011). *Women and banks: Are female customers facing discrimination?* London: Institute for Public Policy Research. Available online at https://www.ippr.org/files/images/media/files/publication/2011/11/womenbanks_Nov2011_8186.pdf (last accessed: February 8, 2021).

Johnson, M. A., Stevenson, R. M., and Letwin, C. R. (2018). A woman's place is in the… startup! Crowdfunder judgments, implicit bias, and the stereotype content model. *Journal of Business Venturing*, *33*(6), 813–831.

Mollick, E., and Robb, A. (2016). Democratizing innovation and capital access: The role of crowdfunding. *California Management Review*, *58*(2), 72–87.

Muravyev, A., Talavera, O., and Schäfer, D. (2009). Entrepreneurs' gender and financial constraints: Evidence from international data. *Journal of Comparative Economics*, *37*(2), 270–286.

Ongena, S., and Popov, A. (2015). *Gender Bias and Credit Access*. ECB Working Paper Series, no. 1822, July 2015.

Zhao, Y., Xie, X., and Yang, L. (2020), Female entrepreneurs and equity crowdfunding: The consequential roles of lead investors and venture stages. *International Entrepreneurship and Management Journal*, 1–29. https://doi.org/10.1007/s11365-020-00659-w

CHAPTER 2

Women in Entrepreneurial Finance: The Academic Perspective

Emanuela Giusi Gaeta

Abstract This chapter is dedicated to examining the scholarly viewpoint about the involvement of women in the domain of entrepreneurial finance. In further depth, it offers a comprehensive analysis of the scholarly literature, encompassing both theoretical frameworks and empirical studies, pertaining to the gender disparity observed in entrepreneurial finance. To this end, it is evident that the gender funding difference in entrepreneurial finance1987 can be attributed to a combination of structural reasons and psychological-social ones, as outlined in Eagly's () social role theory. Afterwards, the chapter examines some recent initiatives undertaken by the European Union (EU) in order to support female entrepreneurship within small and medium-sized enterprises (SMEs).

This work reflects the author's opinions without engaging the Ministry's responsibility. The views expressed in the chapter are those of the author and do not involve the responsibility of the institutions to which she belongs.

F. Battaglia and E. Giusi Gaeta, *Women in Alternative Finance*,
https://doi.org/10.1007/978-3-031-43467-9_2

Keywords Gender gap · Female entrepreneurship · Social role theory · Gender wage discrimination · Gender inequality and structural factor · Business growth and women professional growth · Female funding gap · Policies and cooperation for the gender gap

2.1 The Structural Factors

Gender inequality in credit accessibility is well acknowledged in scholarly discourse and is influenced by a multitude of factors. Existing academic literature on the gender financing gap has primarily concentrated on two primary dimensions, one of which pertains to structural that is the central focus of this section. It is well acknowledged among scholars that gender inequality can be attributed to structural reasons (Ahl 2006; Coleman 2000; Fabowale et al. 1995; Haines et al. 1999; McKechnie et al. 1998). Through the examination of a dataset of 4928 enterprises in the United States, Coleman and Robb (2009) demonstrate that the ability of women to access capital is restricted by both supply and demand constraints. Similarly, Agier and Szafarz (2013) explore a sample of 34,000 micro-loan applications in Brazil and discover the presence of a comparable barrier, commonly referred to as a "glass ceiling". In general, scholarly investigations that centre on structural considerations indicate that enterprises led by women tend to exhibit lower levels of profitability, smaller scales of operation, and slower rates of growth when compared to firms led by men (Du Rietz and Henrekson 2000; Hisrich and Brush 1984; Kalleberg and Leicht 1991; Rosa and Hamilton 1994).

The gender disparity in perceived access to entrepreneurial funding and its evolution in some countries is outlined in the 2016 OECD Report titled "Entrepreneurship at a Glance". The report presents data from 2013 (Fig. 2.1). In all countries, excluding the United States, Mexico, Greece, and Indonesia, there exists a comparable likelihood between men and women in terms of their perceived access to necessary cash for entrepreneurial endeavours. However, it is noteworthy that women tend to exhibit a lower propensity compared to men in disclosing their financial circumstances, as indicated in Fig. 2.1. The observed disparity in gender representation could perhaps be attributed to the presence of less experienced women in industries characterised by high competition or limited growth prospects, gender-based credit assessments, and the influence of gender stereotypes on investment evaluations. Women frequently face disadvantages as a result of restricted availability of fundamental financial services, including checking and savings accounts. Consequently, women entrepreneurs tend to rely on their own funds. Additionally, it is observed that self-employed women exhibit a higher propensity to engage in borrowing activities compared to their self-employed male counterparts. That is someone who refrains from applying for loans due to their perception of poor creditworthiness or doubts regarding the success of their application. Public policies have the potential to enhance women's financial access and mitigate market inefficiencies, such as information asymmetry and inadequate funding. In addition to the prevailing approaches involving the distribution of subsidies, provision of loan guarantees, and implementation of microfinance, there is a nascent public policy initiative that seeks to augment the accessibility of venture capital for women entrepreneurs operating enterprises with an emphasis on expansion and growth. In this regard, new approaches aim to boost the numbers of women in venture capital and business angel networks through targeted recruitment efforts, as well as establishing networks led by women to facilitate investments in firms managed by women. There are also a few initiatives that invest in women-owned businesses in exchange for equity participation.

Upon closer examination, it becomes evident that the United States, despite its reputation for relatively low levels of inequality, exhibits a notable disparity when scrutinising venture capital data sourced from Pitchbook Credit Suisse. This gap pertains specifically to the quantities of financing allocated to individuals based on their gender. Specifically, female entrepreneurs have greater challenges in accessing venture capital investment compared to their male counterparts. There is a lower level of venture capital funding directed towards enterprises run by women. In the European context, it is observed that a technology business supported by venture capital, consisting solely of male founders, attracts a significant majority of the invested capital, amounting to 93%. Conversely, a team with a mixed gender composition obtains a comparatively smaller portion of the capital, accounting for 5%. Furthermore, an all-female team receives the smallest allocation of capital, representing only 2% of the total investment. According to Pitchbook, a financial research business based in the United States, the total funding received by mixed entrepreneurial

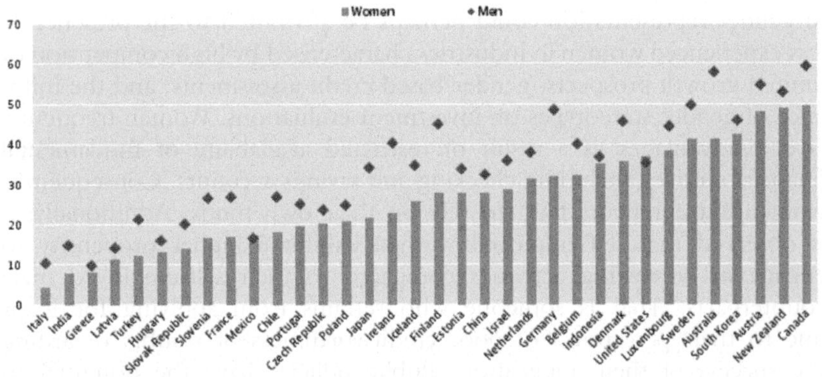

Fig. 2.1 Gender gap in perceived access to entrepreneurship financing and change in gap for selected countries, 2013[1] (*Source* OECD [2016], https://www.oecd.org/gender/data/do-women-have-equal-access-to-finance-for-their-business.htm)

teams in 2020 was estimated to be $23 billion, whereas pure female entrepreneurs earned $3.3 billion in funding. Nevertheless, it is important to acknowledge that there has been an improvement in funding for female venture capital recipients over the course of the last five years, with an increase of 83%. However, it is worth mentioning that this progress has occurred at a slower rate compared to teams consisting of both male and female members, which experienced a funding growth of 95%.

One plausible explanation for the disparity in venture capital investment between women and men is the notable underrepresentation of women in the venture capital ecosystem. This may not come as a surprise, as women tend to run smaller businesses, so ventures targeting companies with revenues of $1 million or more don't need much capital but the all-female team underperformed two other groups, securing only 6% of the funding. This phenomenon prompts further inquiries on the potential influence of other variables, such as potential gender-based biases within the venture capital process. The gender disparity in credit market access can be attributed to many structural causes. Ahl (2006) argues that the assessment of female performance, especially its reliability, is

[1] The percentage of individuals, by gender, who answered "yes" to the question "Do you have access to the money you would need if you wanted to start or grow a business?"

predominantly conducted from a male-centric perspective. The outcomes pertaining to women's access to credit are influenced by historical and cultural circumstances, which can disrupt the results achieved. Sometimes the same gender inequality might be contingent upon another form of gender inequality that exists upstream, such as the varying rates of educational access for women in certain countries. In general, according to the author's perspective, the system necessitates women to conform to the prevailing norms and values. Ahl argues that the acknowledgement of the differences between men and women should not be viewed as a societal drawback, but rather as a progressive step forward, contrary to regressing to previous times. A system that takes gender diversity into account helps society to grow rather than pretend it doesn't exist, which can be a drag on growth. Analysing the nature of loan options and their economic viability for individuals of different genders, it becomes evident that a gap exists in this domain as well. Coleman (2000) highlights how women pay higher interest in the face of greater guarantees and therefore reliability than men. Hence, the inquiry revolves around whether the offer distorts the perception of solvency risk between the two entities, prompting certain scholars to posit that the training of credit agents, specifically lenders, plays a crucial role in rectifying the perception of credit risk solvency disparity between males and females. This, in turn, serves to narrow the gender gap in credit accessibility (Fabowale et al. 1995). According to Coleman and Robb (2009), it is frequently seen that women face the necessity of utilising their own finances, leading to challenges in securing funding, even up to three years after initiating their business ventures. Agier and Szafarz (2013) conducted a survey on 34,000 loan applications from a microfinance company in Brazil. Their findings suggest that the demand for microcredit is skewed towards women, indicating the presence of a potential "glass ceiling" that leads to unequal conditions for women in accessing such credit. Nevertheless, the loan officer's gender is inconsequential in relation to the disparate terms and circumstances associated with the loan that is being granted. In their study conducted in 2000, Du Rietz and Henrekson examined a sample of 4200 entrepreneurs, including 405 women. These entrepreneurs represented a diverse range of economic sectors and had between 1 and 20 employees. The primary objective of the study was to investigate and compare the entrepreneurial performance of men and women. The findings indicate that there is no gender difference in performance in relation to the very small firm, but it emerges in large firms. There is also no difference in profitability between men and women, although the latter seems less interested than men in their growth. Regarding the success and survival rate of male or female businesses, women don't show lower values in terms of success than men, according to a study conducted on 411 companies, belonging to the ICT, food, drink, and health industry, in southern Indiana by Kalleberg and Leicht (1991). In particular, business success depends on differences between industries, organisational structures, and the skills of entrepreneurs. A qualitative survey (Rosa et al. 1996) highlights how there are organisational gender differences: women start an economic activity with a more prudential attitude, that is with fewer activities to carry out than a man, who unlike turns out to be the one who most likely will make use of the financial overdraft. Looking at women's earnings is lower in all sectors, and between men and women, there are differences in roles within the company; many of these did not start without their spouse working full-time and many of them were in public employment. Further, women make more use of business allowance than men who manage to secure other types of financing. In savings levels, there are no gender differences. There is also no discernible disparity in profitability between males and females; however, the latter group appears to exhibit comparatively less enthusiasm towards their personal and professional advancement. In relation to the achievement and viability of businesses owned by individuals of different genders, it has been shown that women do not exhibit lower levels of success compared to men. This finding is based on a comprehensive study undertaken by Kalleberg and Leicht (1991), which examined a sample of 411 enterprises operating in the ICT, food, drink, and health sectors in southern Indiana. The attainment of company success is contingent upon variations among industries, diverse organisational structures, and the proficiencies possessed by entrepreneurs. According to a qualitative survey conducted by Rosa et al. (1996), there are discernible gender differences within organisations. The study reveals that women tend to approach economic activities with a more cautious mindset, engaging in fewer activities compared to men. Conversely, men are more inclined to utilise financial overdrafts as a means of financing their endeavours. The analysis reveals that women consistently experience lower incomes across various sectors. Furthermore, disparities in job positions within organisations are observed between men and women. It is noteworthy that a significant proportion of women's employment trajectories were contingent upon their spouses' full-time employment, and a considerable number of women were engaged in public sector employment. Moreover, it has been observed that women tend to utilise business allowances to a greater extent compared to men, who often rely on alternative forms of funding. There is no discernible disparity between genders in terms of savings levels.

2.2 The Psychological-Social Factors

The subsequent body of scholarship pertaining to the examination of the gender financing disparity centres around the social role theory developed by Eagly (1987). This idea posits that individuals are compelled to cultivate specific stereotypes to attain social acceptance. Certain stereotypes are ascribed based on an individual's gender. Gender stereotypes encompass preconceived notions and prior judgements that carry substantial emotional weight and mirror societal perceptions of men and women. These stereotypes tend to associate males with a greater inclination towards domains of achievement and assertiveness, while females are often associated with care-oriented behaviours and docility.

The hypothesis presented in this study is grounded on the examination of gender patterns, which are influenced by societal norms dictating proper behaviours for both women and men (Eagly 1987; Eagly and Carli 2003; López-Zafra et al. 2009). Specifically, in many societies, there exists a prevailing societal norm that assigns women the primary role of managing domestic affairs, including household chores and the nurturing of children and older family members. Conversely, men are typically expected to engage in paid employment to financially sustain the family unit. Hence, it can be observed that the male demographic is commonly perceived as the preferred archetype for initiating and managing entrepreneurial ventures (Bird and Brush 2002), but women often encounter obstacles when attempting to capitalise on economic prospects (Carter and Rosa 1998). Other authors, like Connell (1990), argue that the gender-related stereotypes of the individual derive from what he calls "hegemonic masculinity". This concept relies on hegemonic which examines the societal positioning of males through various patterns, actions, beliefs, and discourses that enable them to acquire and sustain an advantageous position relative to women (Connell and Messerschmidt 2005).

Psychological factors represent a particular component in elucidating the variations in biodiversity observed between men and women.

However, prior to delving into the literature's findings on the reasons of the gender gap, it is necessary to examine a set of established observations that can aid in comprehending the significant role played by psychological factors in influencing disparities in performance between males and females. The stylised facts correlate the level of development between countries and the gender gap, also scrutinising what happens inside the home, to understand how stereotypes, preconceptions, and divisions of tasks arise and at the same time, impact the psychological factor that divides men and women, in terms of opportunities in the labour market.

The differences between men and women in the labour market have long been a hotly debated topic in the literature. The level of economic development does not eliminate gender disparities, as industrialised economies, especially in some areas, accentuate this phenomenon. In this regard, it may be interesting to observe what happens, for example, at the G7 level. The "G7 Dashboard on Gender Gaps" (OECD 2022a, b, c) overlooks the phenomenon of the gender gap in terms of access to the labour market. With the dashboard, the G7 is engaged in implementing a recommendation of the G7 Gender Equality Advisory Council and Women (GEAC[2]). This provides an important new tool to support the G7's efforts to achieve gender equality and to monitor progress continuously. The G7 project on the gender gap involves the G7 countries that provide their own calculations that they are compared at G7 and OECD levels. Data is annually updated by OECD. Figure 2.2 presents an analysis of Italy's calculations, focusing on its cultural stiffness in comparison with the German countries within the G7 European nations. Italy is identified as a country with more pronounced cultural rigidity, while being economically advanced. The comparison between Italy and Germany is primarily invoked in instances where a counterfactual concept is required. The aforementioned approach is similarly employed when drawing a comparison with the United States, in order to gain insight into international occurrences and juxtapose the data with a nation characterised by both advanced economic development and a greater receptiveness to free market principles, while being less influenced by cultural inflexibilities.

[2] The Advisory Council become hooked up in 2017 to champion gender equality and recommend wherein greater motion is wanted to address continual inequality, assist ladies in work, give up violence in opposition to young ladies and ladies, and venture gender stereotypes.

Based on the analysis of Figs. 2.2 and 2.3, it is evident that there is a discernible trend of the wage gap between men and women gradually decreasing. This pattern is consistently observed across various countries and demographic groups. However, it is noteworthy that the gender gap appears to be more pronounced in the highly industrialised nations constituting the G7, particularly among those adhering to the OECD. This suggests a potential negative association between the level of industrialisation and the extent of the gender gap, possibly becoming more prominent beyond a certain threshold—presumably, starting from a particular phase of development. In any event, when considering the comparison of the indicator's value within individual countries, specifically Italy and Germany, it is evident that the level of development has a detrimental effect on the gender wage gap. This is substantiated by the fact that in Germany, women earn a salary that is 13.9% lower than men, whereas in Italy, this disparity amounts to 7.6%. In conclusion, it appears that the influence of Italian cultural rigidities on the gender wage gap is not as significant as the impact of economic development. Theoretically, economic development should result in a reduction of this disparity, as emphasised by the literature referenced in Sect. 2.1.

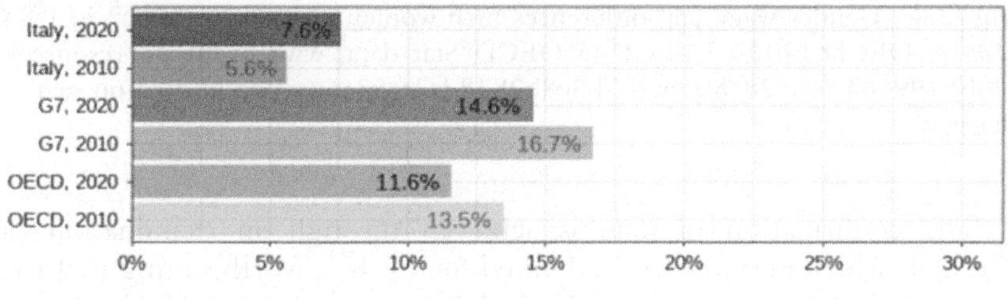

Fig. 2.2 Gender wage gap differences men-women (relative to men)[3] in Italy (*Source* OECD [2022b] based on OECD Stat data, https://www.g7germany.de/resource/blob/974430/2058170/3f90a9cb877a250f56245ede5adbf53a/2022-06-28-gender-gap-italy-data.pdf?download=1)

[3] The indicator is defined as the unadjusted difference between the median wages of men and women. Median wages for men are based on total earnings for full-time employees. There are weakly earnings data relative to earnings pay for Canada, UK, and USA, while monthly data for France, Germany, Italy, and Japan. Data of France, Germany, and Italy refer to 2018.

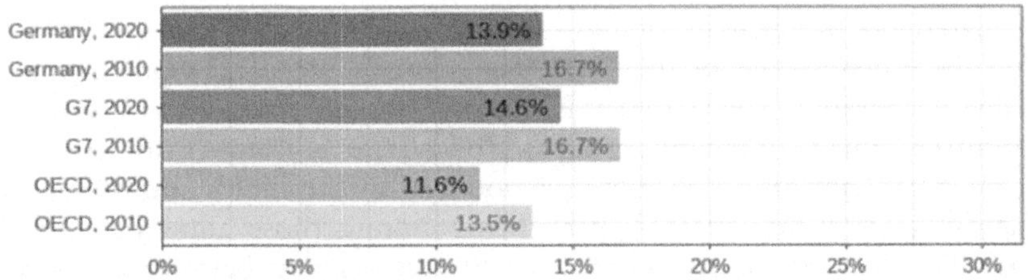

Fig. 2.3 Gender wage gap differences men-women (relative to men)[4] in Germany (*Source* OECD [2022a] based on OECD Stat data, https://www.g7germany.de/resource/blob/974430/2058072/5eafec9454770407b4f5719778ff7f50/2022-06-28-gender-gap-germany-data.pdf?download=1)

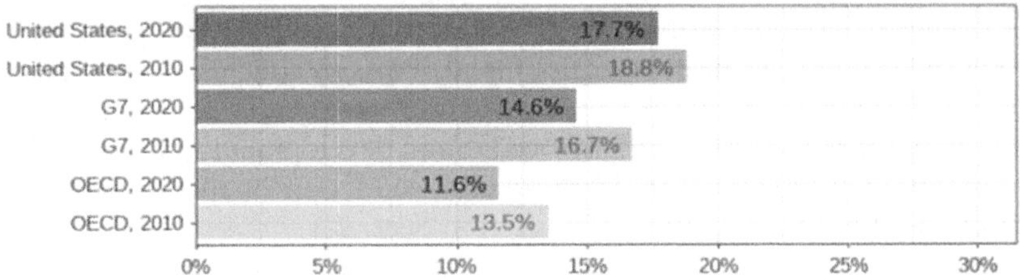

Fig. 2.4 Gender wage gap differences men-women (relative to men)[5] in USA (*Source* OECD [2022c] based on OECD Stat data, www.bmfsfj.de/resource/blob/199066/66728e8bae6287b5e8b2848d41fe53a6/g7-dashboard-on-gender-gaps-usa-data.pdf)

The confirmation of data is achieved through an examination of Fig. 2.4, which pertains to the United States. It is worth noting that the earnings data for Canada, the United Kingdom, and the United States

[4] The indicator is defined as the unadjusted difference between the median wages of men and women. Median wages for men are based on total earnings for full-time employees. There are weakly earnings data relative to earnings pay for Canada, UK, and USA, while monthly data for France, Germany, Italy, and Japan. Data of France, Germany, and Italy refer to 2018.

[5] The indicator is defined as the unadjusted difference between the median wages of men and women. Median wages for men are based on total earnings for full-time employees. There are weakly earnings data relative to earnings pay for Canada, UK, and USA, while monthly data for France, Germany, Italy, and Japan. Data of France, Germany, and Italy refer to 2018.

exhibits a certain degree of weakness in comparison with earnings pay. Conversely, monthly data is available for France, Germany, Italy, and Japan. The data pertaining to France, Germany, and Italy pertains to the year 2018, as shown in footnote 2.

Even looking at unpaid jobs, there is a disparity in the amount of time allocated by men and women might be observed (Fig. 2.5). Specifically, there is a notable discrepancy in the allocation of time spent on household chores between men and women, with men generally dedicating less time to such tasks. This inequality is particularly pronounced in Italy when compared to other countries within the G7. Nevertheless, a discrepancy exists among countries and the Organisation for Economic Co-operation and Development (OECD). In this instance, the data favours the more developed nations, as they demonstrate a greater degree of containment. This can be attributed to the G7's political commitment to achieving gender equality in the distribution of unpaid labour, as a prerequisite for

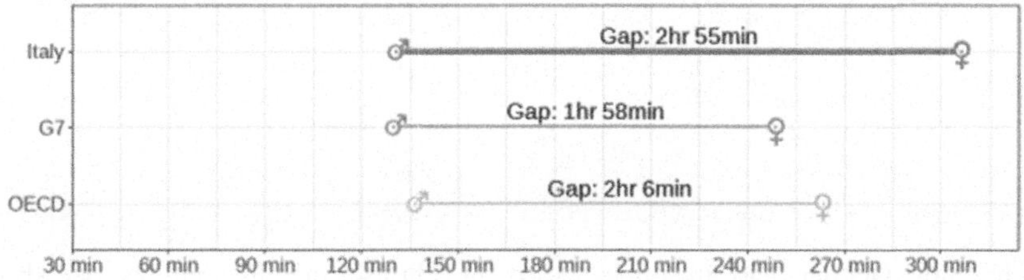

Fig. 2.5 Gender gap in unpaid care and housework in minutes per day (women♀, men♂)[6] in Italy (*Source* OECD [2022b] based on OECD Stat data, https://www.g7germany.de/resource/blob/974430/2058170/3f90a9cb877a250f56245ede5adbf53a/2022-06-28-gender-gap-italy-data.pdf?download=1)

[6] Defined as the time spent on unpaid work out of total available time per day. Days from 15 to 64 years old. Time spent on unpaid work includes: shopping; caring for family; children caring; adult care; caring for people outside the family; independent work; travel related to household chores; Other Unpaid Activities. Country results are not always perfectly comparable due to the different classifications of time use in individual countries. No trends are shown due to large differences between survey years. 2019 data for Japan and US, 2019 data for 2015 Canada and UK 2014, Italy 2013, Germany 2013, France 2011. OECD average is OECD-30 Average excluding Chile, Colombia, Costa Rica, Czech Republic, Iceland, Israel, Slovak Republic, and Switzerland. EU The average is the EU20 average, excluding all non-OECD EU member countries and the Czech and Slovak Republics.

participating in the Gender Equality Advisory (GEA) initiative. In any circumstance, there exists a disparity in the division of domestic labour, which becomes further pronounced when there is a clear delineation of responsibilities within the household. Italy, among the G7 nations, has a notable disparity in the division of household labour between males and females, which can be attributed to cultural factors and social organisational frameworks. Examining the data for Germany and the USA (Figs. 2.6 and 2.7), it becomes evident that in economically advanced nations with fewer cultural constraints, the gender gap in unpaid domestic labour is less pronounced. Specifically, Germany exhibits a relatively lower level of inequity compared to the USA, whereas Italy demonstrates a significantly higher disparity when compared to these two nations.

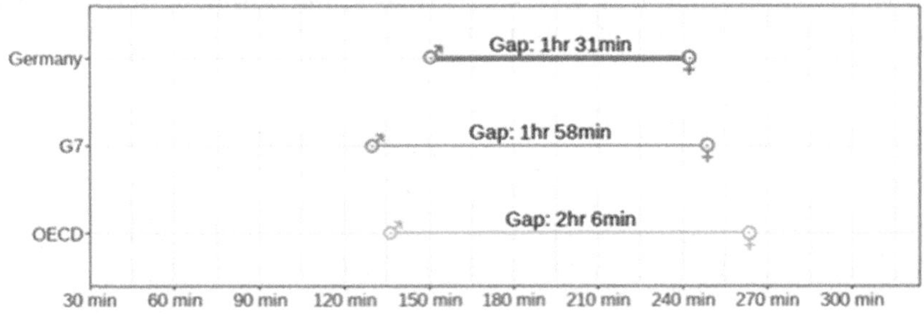

Fig. 2.6 Gender gap in unpaid care and housework in minutes per day (women♀, men♂)[7] in Germany (*Source* OECD [2022a] based on OECD Stat data, https://www.g7germany.de/resource/blob/974430/2058072/5eafec9454770407b4f5719778ff7f50/2022-06-28-gender-gap-germany-data.pdf?download=1)

[7] Defined as the time spent on unpaid work out of total available time per day. Days from 15 to 64 years old. Time spent on unpaid work includes: shopping; caring for family; children caring; adult care; caring for people outside the family; independent work; travel related to household chores; Other Unpaid Activities. Country results are not always perfectly comparable due to the different classifications of time use in individual countries. No trends are shown due to large differences between survey years. 2019 data for Japan and US, 2019 data for 2015 Canada and UK 2014, Italy 2013, Germany 2013, France 2011. OECD average is OECD-30 Average excluding Chile, Colombia, Costa Rica, Czech Republic, Iceland, Israel, Slovak Republic, and Switzerland. EU The average is the EU20 average, excluding all non-OECD EU member countries and the Czech and Slovak Republics.

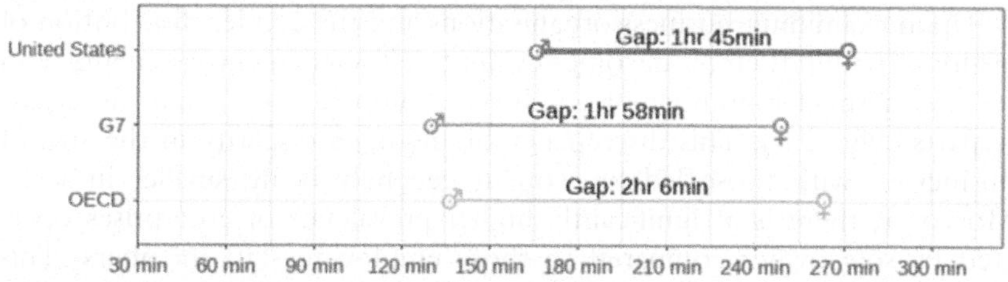

Fig. 2.7 Gender gap in unpaid care and housework in minutes per day (women♀ men♂)[8] in USA (*Source* OECD [2022c] based on OECD Stat data, www.bmfsfj.de/resource/blob/199066/66728e8bae6287b5e8b2848d41fe53a6/g7-dashboard-on-gender-gaps-usa-data.pdf)

Based on the referenced OECD data, it is evident that the G7 nations saw a negligible disparity in pension income between genders for the year 2020. However, when we look at business organisations and the roles occupied by women and men, we immediately notice that women entrepreneurs have fewer employees than men, revealing differences also in the size of the business, which is smaller if run by women. Moreover, the prevalence of enterprises operated by single-owner entrepreneurs surpasses that of businesses employing staff members. This observation holds true for individuals of all genders, as depicted in Fig. 2.4.

[8] Defined as the time spent on unpaid work out of total available time per day. Days from 15 to 64 years old. Time spent on unpaid work includes: shopping; caring for family; children caring; adult care; caring for people outside the family; independent work; travel related to household chores; Other Unpaid Activities. Country results are not always perfectly comparable due to the different classifications of time use in individual countries. No trends are shown due to large differences between survey years. 2019 data for Japan and US, 2019 data for 2015 Canada and UK 2014, Italy 2013, Germany 2013, France 2011. OECD average is OECD-30 Average excluding Chile, Colombia, Costa Rica, Czech Republic, Iceland, Israel, Slovak Republic, and Switzerland. EU The average is the EU20 average, excluding all non-OECD EU member countries and the Czech and Slovak Republics.

Upon examining business organisations and the gender distribution of positions within them, it becomes evident that women entrepreneurs tend to have a smaller number of employees compared to their male counterparts (Fig. 2.8). This discrepancy highlights a disparity in the size of businesses, with those led by women generally being smaller in scale. Moreover, there is a significantly higher prevalence of enterprises operated by sole owner compared to those employing staff members. This assertion holds true for individuals of both genders. If we look at the percentage distribution of women occupying the position of Chair of Boards of Directors in the largest and most important companies listed on the stock exchange (Fig. 2.9), it becomes evident that there persists a disparity in the level of participation between men and women. This disparity has shown a gradual decline over the period from 2016 to 2021. However, as of 2021, slightly more than 30% of women hold top executive positions in listed companies, while in OECD countries, the proportion is slightly lower. According to the OECD research, there remains a substantial amount of work to be accomplished at the policy level for the industrialised countries that have been assessed thus far. Based on the observations depicted in Figs. 2.9, 2.10, and 2.11, it appears that there is a positive correlation between the level of economic growth and the gender disparity observed in high-level entrepreneurial positions. The United States has the lowest percentage of women in power in the largest, publicly traded companies, in comparison with Germany and Italy.

Analysing the assistance provided to address gender disparities in Italy and by members of the Development Assistance Committee (DAC), it becomes evident that the primary aid (referred to as GE1) consistently surpasses the most significant help (referred to as GE2), indicating that while closing the gender gap remains a priority, it is considered a secondary objective. The disparity in the forms of assistance provided by development cooperation funds is significant between GE2 and GE1. Consequently, at the policy level, there remains a substantial amount of work to be accomplished for the industrialised nations that have been investigated thus far. This conclusion is derived from the report published by the OECD. However, when comparing the amount of aid received by Italy-Germany and the USA in relation to GE2, it becomes evident that the former country received a greater amount of assistance compared

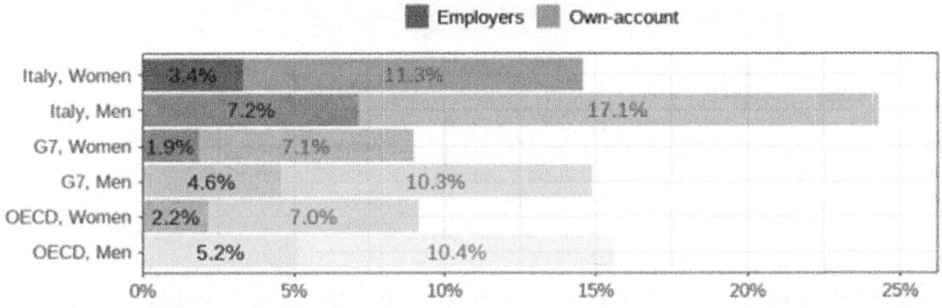

Fig. 2.8 Share of self-employed with and without employees among all employed in Italy, 2019[9] (*Source* OECD [2022b] based on OECD Stat data, https://www.g7germany.de/resource/blob/974430/2058170/3f90a9cb877a250f56245ede5adbf53a/2022-06-28-gender-gap-italy-data.pdf?download=1)

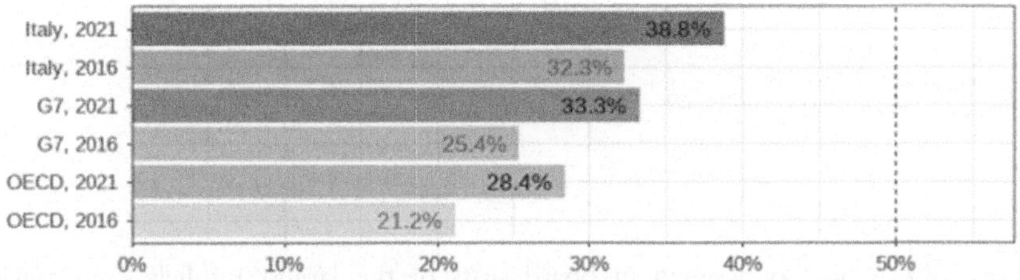

Fig. 2.9 Share of women in board seats of the largest public companies[10] in Italy (*Source* OECD [2022b] based on OECD Stat data, https://www.g7germany.de/resource/blob/974430/2058170/3f90a9cb877a250f56245ede5adbf53a/2022-06-28-gender-gap-italy-data.pdf?download=1)

[9] Defined as the percentage of all employees registered as self-employed, whether they have employees or not, they are further classified. In some countries, registered self-employed persons are partly or not included in the number of self-employed persons. This may affect comparability country. The data covers the aged 15–64, while the US covers everyone aged 16 and over. Data related until 2019.

[10] Indicator defined as the percentage of women in the highest decision-making bodies decision-making bodies of their respective companies. A Board of Directors of a Single Company or, in the case of a two-tier system, a supervisory board. For EU countries, data refers to top 50 members of a country's leading blue chips index (includes only companies registered in that country). Data for non-EU countries is for companies that are included in the MSCI ACWI index, with management and audit committees omitted.

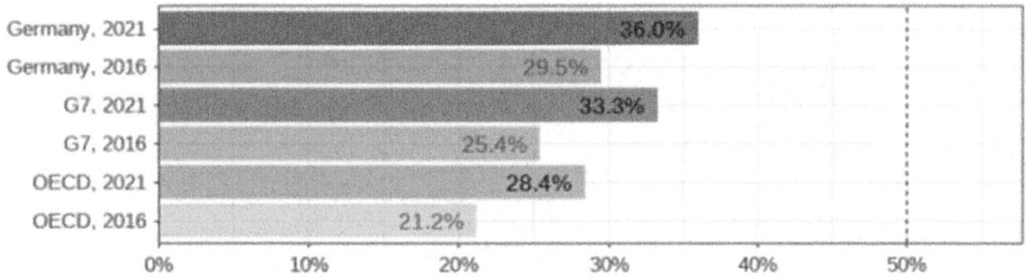

Fig. 2.10 Share of women in board seats of the largest public companies. Germany (*Source* OECD [2022a] based on OECD Stat data, https://www.g7germany.de/resource/blob/974430/2058072/5eafec9454770407b4f5719778ff7f50/2022-06-28-gender-gap-germany-data.pdf?download=1)

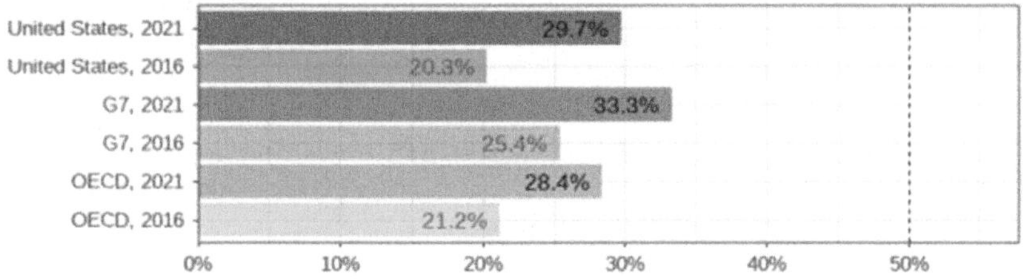

Fig. 2.11 Share of women in board seats of the largest publicly companies in USA (*Source* OECD [2022a] based on OECD Stat data, https://www.g7germany.de/resource/blob/974430/2058072/5eafec9454770407b4f5719778ff7f50/2022-06-28-gender-gap-germany-data.pdf?download=1)

to the other nations (see Figs. 2.12, 2.13 and 2.14). Specifically, Italy-Germany received twice the amount of aid as the USA and three times the amount of aid as Germany. In the context of GE1 (see Figs. 2.12, 2.13, and 2.14), it appears that the United States has made limited progress in addressing gender inequality, as it does not prioritise this issue. Italy was one of the three countries that received the highest amount of aid in relation to gender equality (GE). This could also be attributed to the presence of a more pronounced gender gap in other dimensions of the labour market, which were not specifically analysed in the OECD report. It would be intriguing to incorporate an indicator into the G7 Dashboard that provides a concise overview of the political initiatives undertaken to address the gender gap, and subsequently compare these efforts with the corresponding aid received.

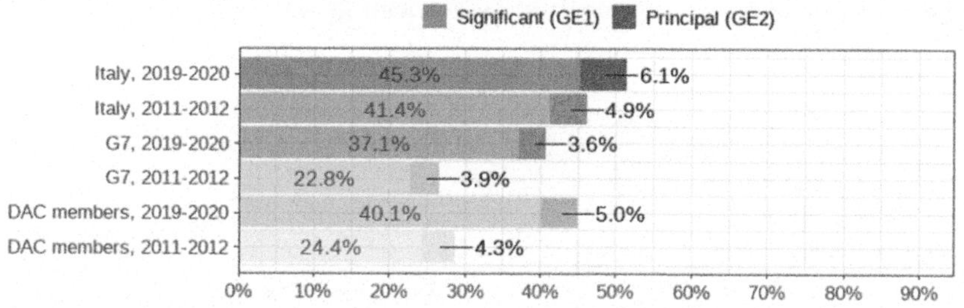

Fig. 2.12 Funds for development cooperation (GE1 and GE2)[11] in Italy (*Source* OECD [2022b] based on OECD Stat data, https://www.g7germany.de/resource/blob/974430/2058170/3f90a9cb877a250f56245ede5adbf53a/2022-06-28-gender-gap-italy-data.pdf?download=1)

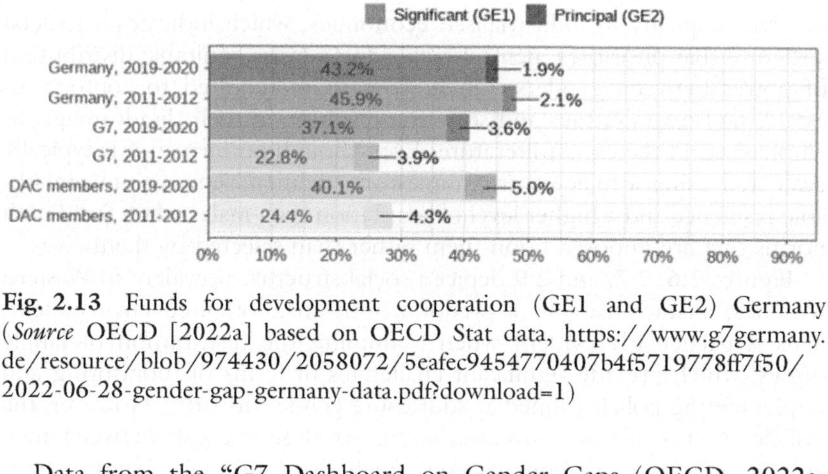

Fig. 2.13 Funds for development cooperation (GE1 and GE2) Germany (*Source* OECD [2022a] based on OECD Stat data, https://www.g7germany.de/resource/blob/974430/2058072/5eafec9454770407b4f5719778ff7f50/2022-06-28-gender-gap-germany-data.pdf?download=1)

Data from the "G7 Dashboard on Gender Gaps (OECD, 2022a, b, c)" reports based on OECD. The Stat data reveals the presence of

[11] Data pertains to the proportion of commitments related to gender equality within all evaluated bilateral official development assistance (ODA) pledges. Primary commitments (referred to as GE2) prioritise gender equality as a clear and foundational aim of the initiative, while significant commitments (labelled GE1) view gender equality as a crucial but secondary goal. The information regarding commitments for the empowerment of women and gender equality is gathered annually through the OECD Creditor Reporting System (CRS) utilising the OECD Development Assistance Committee (DAC) gender equality policy indicator. These commitments are showcased as two-year averages in constant 2019 USD, given their potential fluctuation from one year to the next.

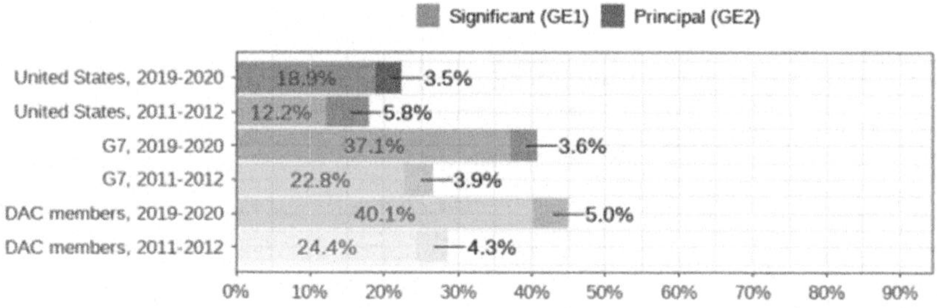

Fig. 2.14 Funds for development cooperation (GE1 and GE2)_USA (*Source* OECD [2022a] based on OECD Stat data, https://www.g7germany.de/resource/blob/974430/2058072/5eafec9454770407b4f5719778ff7f50/2022-06-28-gender-gap-germany-data.pdf?download=1)

gender inequality in industrialised economies, which indicates a societal structure that prioritises men overachieving a more equitable distribution of power between genders. Often women are required to conform to established organisations and societies, resulting in their disadvantage, as emphasised in the extant literature. Even though performance is typically evaluated using a male-centric framework, women demonstrate remarkable resilience and a higher level of adaptation than males when faced with norms that are imposed upon them rather than selected by themselves.

Figures 2.6, 2.7, and 2.9 depict a social structure prevalent in Western societies, characterised by a predominantly male-oriented environment. This is particularly evident when examining the distribution of family duties, which provide significant challenges in terms of monitoring and implementing policies aimed at addressing gender disparity. However, the policies themselves are also insufficient to close the gap between men and women in the labour market. Each firm, to some extent, serves as a microcosm of the macroeconomic landscape, where gender disparities manifest through several points of view. Biologists assert that gender differences are a result of gonadal and other sex-specific hormones. The disparities seen by sociologists can be attributed to the varying social positions occupied by men and women within larger social hierarchies. The disparity observed among economists can be attributed to variations in the human capital possessed by individuals of different genders. Development researchers arise from gender-related temperament and socialisation experiences. Evolutionary psychologists typically advocate for the influence of selection forces with potential gender biases on the ancestral development of humans. In the "Social Role Theory" (Eagly 1987), there is a unique socio-psychological perspective that emphasises social roles and interweaves role-related processes with these other perspectives to create a powerful analysis of gender differences and similarities. In summary, the presence of gender disparities and shared behaviours can be attributed to the influence of gender role beliefs, which in turn are shaped by individuals' perceptions of the societal expectations placed upon men and women within their respective communities. For example, in post-industrial cultures, there exists a notable disparity in employment patterns between men and women, with men being more inclined towards securing employment, particularly in authoritative roles, while women tend to assume a greater share of domestic and professional obligations. The categorisation of individuals into distinct social roles is influenced by the physical disparities that arise from human gender differentiation. Given these physical differences, specific tasks are executed with greater efficiency by individuals of different genders, contingent upon prevailing social circumstances and cultural norms. Consequently, this phenomenon engenders the formation of a division of labour alliance.

Traits attribute to men and women who prepare for gender-typical roles. These attributes are reflected in consensual common beliefs and gender stereotypes. In everyday life, people recognise these gender roles by taking on specific social roles such as parents and employees. They seem natural and inevitable because gender roles seem to reflect the innate attributes of gender. With these beliefs, people construct gender roles that correspond to cultural and environmental conditions, but which appear to individuals within society as stable, inherent characteristics of men and women, and Widely socialise society to develop personality traits and skills that facilitate the performance of roles. Furthermore, gender roles influence behaviour through biological and psychological processes. These proximal causes in human female behaviour involve biological processes including hormonal changes and sociocultural factors such as gender identity and stereotypical expectations. These three factors not only interact to achieve gender differences but also similarities. The significance of Eagly's thesis resides in its establishment of a theoretical framework for comprehending gender variation, specifically within the realm of psychology, as a contributing cause to the distinctions observed between males and females. The inclusion of gender gap possibilities has facilitated the advancement of scholarly writing by enabling the exploration of distinct dimensions of gender disparity. In the 1980s, the notion of masculinity saw significant cultural proliferation, representing a pinnacle of growth within the twentieth century. This particular situation has resulted in the emergence of organisational structures that exhibit a growing inclination towards masculinity, alongside the simultaneous rise of feminist groups that are becoming more critical and assertive. The outcome included a global context necessitating a collective agreement, exemplified by the temporary abolition of the abortion ban, which was subsequently reinstated in the United States within a brief period. Simultaneously, in the year 2022, two women ascend to positions of governmental authority as Prime Ministers of Italy and the United Kingdom. However, it is noteworthy that Italy's appointment of a female Prime Minister marks the initial occurrence of such an event in the country, indicating a significant societal transformation. The finding is substantiated in a study conducted by Eagly and Carli (2003), which suggests that women have undergone transformations in terms of their educational attainment and subsequent entry into the workforce. As a result, they are now capable of occupying significant positions within organisations and in some cases, even assuming leadership roles at the national level. This outcome serves to challenge traditional gender norms and establish a precedent for future advancements. According to the authors, the increase in appointments of women at the top of society has contributed to the change of society more in favour of a gender balance. The stylised facts cited that see two premier women in the same year and highlight how forces with different directions are in place on the way of conceiving the organisation of social life, more masculine or feminine or simply more balanced. Per Bird and Brush (2002), women have exerted an influence on the establishment and organisational structure of businesses. Entrepreneurs can be assessed not only based on their level of success, but also on their decision-making on the allocation of time between work and leisure, which may vary between men and women. Additionally, entrepreneurs can be evaluated on their ability to develop their workforce, such as through training initiatives, in order to mitigate the risk of losing experienced employees. In this particular scenario, there exists a divergence between men and women in terms of their decision-making processes, as well as the allocation of resources towards philanthropic endeavours and humanitarian assistance in a broader context. Additionally, disparities may be observed in their levels of sensitivity towards environmental concerns. In the present study, the researchers differentiate gender maturity, which refers to the capacity to discern distinctions between males and females, from gender balance, which pertains to disparities in opportunities rather than inherent traits of the two genders. The incorporation of these two concepts in the research will enhance comprehension of the gender gap issue, hence facilitating the implementation of more effective strategies to address it.

Nevertheless, there are some who argue that rather than eliminating the notion of masculinity altogether, it should be included and assimilated into a broader framework. According to Connell and Messerschmidt (2005), it is proposed that models based on the male metric should be integrated with a geographical dimension. This integration would involve examining the interactions between local, regional, and global contexts to identify areas where male models dominate, leading to gender disparities. The distribution of top positions between men and women should be closely observed to better understand this issue. Additionally, it is important to address the contradictions inherent in male models and strive for greater gender democracy. As stated by Connell (2009), there exists a restricted representation of women in the political sphere, which has resulted in structural implications for a society that is skewed towards masculinity rather than achieving a balanced gender distribution. However, women have discovered alternate avenues to express their opinions by means of feminist groups, which challenge male-dominated political agendas. This has resulted in a shift in political aims, as society continues to evolve and strive for gender equality. Hence, the author posits that the involvement of the state is of paramount importance in achieving gender equilibrium. However, considering this assertion, it is imperative to reconsider the function of the state in a more intricate manner, incorporating a heightened level of gender interaction that may effectively alleviate gender disparities. In essence, the literature that examines the gender gap through a psychological lens provides valuable insights, shedding light on how psychological disparities between males and females can have significant global implications. This is particularly evident in the context of entrepreneurial endeavours, where individual variances, including psychological factors, shape business decisions. However, it is important to note that these choices should not be automatically equated with the notion of "Think manager, think male" (Schein and Davidson 1993).

2.2.1 *Empirical Evidence on Gender Funding Gap in Entrepreneurial Finance*

This section presents a detailed analysis of the primary results from available research that specifically examines the financing gap experienced by female entrepreneurs. This study presents compelling evidence indicating that women face significant disadvantages compared to men in various funding markets. Previous research has demonstrated this gender disparity private equity (e.g. Becker-Blease and Sohl 2007), institutional capital (e.g. Bigelow et al. 2014b), and bank financing (e.g. Eddleston et al. 2016; Ongena and Popov 2015; Alesina et al. 2013; Hertz 2011; Muravyev et al. 2009; Fay and Williams 1993; Buttner and Rosen 1988).

There exists a significant body of information indicating that women face disadvantages compared to males in many financing markets. In order to contextualise this issue, we will initially analyse relevant statistics. Subsequently, we will explore the existing literature's attempts to provide explanations for this phenomenon. There are a limited number of reports that provide analysis on the intricacies of financing through bank loans, institutional capital, and private equity. However, the International Financing Corporation (IFC)[12] Report (2021) takes a fairly detailed picture of gender discrimination financing for private equity, venture capital, and portfolio companies. The primary focus of this research pertains to developing markets, aligning with the strategic emphasis of the International Finance Corporation (IFC) on this subject matter. If the assertion that there are challenges in funding women's projects in developed nations holds true, this notion becomes even more applicable when considering projects in emerging markets. Consequently, an examination is conducted to gauge the extent of gender inequality in funding, by comparing the findings from the International Finance Corporation (IFC), which indicate that only 7% of private equity and venture capital investments are directed towards companies led by women.

The firm that is predominantly controlled by women received just 65% of the total funding it received. A corporation of moderate size

[12] IFC is the institution of the World Bank Group with the purpose to support private investments in developing countries. A sister organization of the World Bank and a member of the World Bank Group, it is the world's largest development institution focused on the private sector in emerging markets. It works with 2,000 and more companies around the world, using its capital, expertise, and influence to create markets and opportunities in the world's most challenging places.

managed by male individuals. The primary explanation for this disparity can be attributed to the higher representation of women. Organisations have the potential to secure additional financial resources during its first phases, particularly through avenues like accelerators and incubators. The investment scale has a lesser magnitude in comparison with the latter stage, particularly in cases when the investment amount is substantial. A potential factor contributing to this bias might be the somewhat lower likelihood of female-led enterprises securing subsequent rounds of investment compared to their male-led counterparts. The percentage comparison between 13% and 17% is being considered. Furthermore, it is possible to provide a more comprehensive explanation. This finding may be associated with the correlation between the frequency of female CEOs who get their initial fundraising round and the subsequent likelihood of being replaced by male leaders in later rounds. Approximately 20% of the firms in the portfolio exhibit a state of gender balance across their leadership teams. Approximately 70% of the population consists of males. It has been demonstrated that emerging market private equity and venture capital funds exhibit a preference for investing in leadership teams that are both gender balanced and limited in number, contrary to prevailing notions. According to the findings of the study, participants saw that decision-making was enhanced in teams that exhibited gender balance. Enhancing diversity within governance structures can lead to improved governance practices and facilitate the expansion of consumer reach in bigger markets. Leadership teams that are gender balanced have a higher probability of receiving money compared to teams that are unbalanced in terms of gender. The possibility of receiving funds is larger by a factor of 25 for gender-balanced teams. The valuation of portfolio firms had a significant increase of 64% during the transition between two rounds of liquidity events or funding.

According to data obtained from the World Bank Development Indicators, it is evident that a significant proportion of Chinese enterprises, namely 64%, exhibit female participation. This figure surpasses the average female participation rate seen in the second-best performing area, Latin America and Caribbean Countries (LAC), by a notable margin of 33%. The phenomenon of increased female leadership in China persists among both General Partners and portfolio firms. China has witnessed the emergence of several private equity/venture capital firms that are helmed by women. Notably, as of 2010, five out of the past nine unicorn businesses started by women have originated in China. This particular nation stands out as the sole developing market economy with a noteworthy presence of numerous unicorns run by female entrepreneurs. The data from the International Finance Corporation (IFC) indicates a noteworthy disparity in the turnover rate of female CEOs compared to their male counterparts. The findings suggest that female CEOs have a somewhat lower likelihood of being affirmed in subsequent rounds, leading to a substitution with a male CEO. Moreover, it has been shown that a mere 13% of firms led by female chief executive officers (CEOs) obtain substantial refinancing of investments, while their male counterparts experience a higher rate of 17%. Nevertheless, the impact of subsequent fundraising rounds on firms has been significant. The phenomenon of male CEOs replacing female CEOs in succession has been shown to influence the outcome of the first transaction. According to available data, around 31% of firms are led by female chief executive officers (CEOs). However, it has been observed that in cases when these enterprises secure a subsequent round of funding, there is a tendency for female CEOs to be replaced by their male counterparts. Approximately 50% of such instances involve the original Chief Executive Officer (CEO) having some form of affiliation with the firm or assuming the role of CEO. In the subsequent funding round, the former Managing Director, who is also a Co-Founder or Co-CEO, may still be recognised in their previous role, but will not be acknowledged as a member of the board. The occurrence of gender disparity in CEO appointments is evident, as just 2% of CEOs in the initial round of investment were women. While the available data indicates a potential bias against women entrepreneurs in securing subsequent funding rounds, such as through CEO replacements, it is essential to gather more gender-specific data over an extended period to conduct a comprehensive evaluation.

The management of Portfolio/Venture capital businesses in developing economies is characterised by a predominant presence of male-dominated teams. According to the investigation conducted by the International Finance Corporation (IFC), it was found that teams with a gender balance accounted for a mere 19% of the overall composition. The senior leadership of the portfolio company consisted of teams that were mostly male, with all-male teams comprising 68% and male-dominated teams comprising 12%. There are notable disparities within developing market regions in terms of gender-balanced leadership within organisations. Specifically, the Eastern Europe and Central Asia (ECA) region has a higher proportion, with 29% of companies exhibiting gender balance in their leadership positions. In contrast, the South Asia region displays a comparatively lower percentage, with only 13% of companies achieving gender balance in their leadership roles. There is a noticeable discrepancy between the gender composition of a firm's top management and its predominantly male investor base, with the former displaying a greater degree of gender balance. This imbalance is particularly pronounced in developing economies, where women occupying senior positions in top management account for a mere 28%. The findings from the International Finance Corporation (IFC) indicate that investment funds overseen by teams with a gender balance had superior performance compared to teams that were mostly composed of either men or women. This outperformance was shown specifically in the context of developing markets and investment strategies. Additionally, venture capital is encompassed within this context. Investments exhibit a tendency to be concentrated inside the technology sector. Women tend to exhibit lower levels of labour force involvement compared to males in the overall market. Furthermore, as an illustration, an investment strategy exhibits an average excess return in the realm of venture capital that surpasses 4.5 percentage points. Similarly, it demonstrates a greater excess return in growth capital buyouts, above 1.6%, as well as in real assets, surpassing 1.3 percentage points. Moreover, it has been observed that investment funds overseen by teams with a balanced representation of genders have exhibited superior performance compared to teams that are mostly composed of either men or women, particularly in the context of emerging markets and investment strategies.

Following a look at gender disparities across various companies, encompassing diverse geographical locations and levels of market development, with a specific emphasis on the distribution of genders within funding roles, it becomes pertinent to explore how scholarly literature addresses the inequities pertaining to access to various funding sources, including angel capital. The existing literature has examined women's utilisation of debt finance and venture capital, although there is a dearth of knowledge on women's access to cash from private individual investors, sometimes referred to as business angels. According to the argument put out by Freear and Wetzel (1992), angelic capital plays a crucial role in the initial phase of securing venture capital or can serve as a feasible alternative during the early stage. Risk capital refers to the financial resources that are allocated to investment opportunities with a higher degree of uncertainty and potential for loss. Therefore, it is crucial to ascertain the level of access that women entrepreneurs have to this significant capital resource. In a scholarly article, Becker-Blease and Sohl (2007) explore the issue of gender equality in accessing angel capital. The authors examine potential disparities between male and female entrepreneurs in terms of their pursuit and acquisition of angel capital. Additionally, they investigate whether there is evidence of sex-based biases, such as homophilia, in the process of searching for and evaluating potential recipients of angel capital. The authors also examine the potential disparity between women and men in terms of relinquishing ownership of their enterprises in return for additional funding. The research conducted by the authors offers significant empirical support for the existence of gender differences in access to and involvement within the heavenly capital market, a crucial avenue of financial funding. This study utilises yearly angelic capital data that was allocated to several organisations throughout the period from 2000 to 2004. Empirical research demonstrates that female entrepreneurs are allocated a disproportionately small fraction of the overall angelic capital. Nevertheless, the findings of this study indicate a rather low proportion of women actively pursuing angel capital investment, since just 8.9% of the proposals originate from female entrepreneurs. This study also investigates the influence of sex homophily on research activities and the allocation of angel financing. In particular, the authors verify whether women are more active than men in seeking angelic capital investments than men and therefore are also the ones most likely to receive this type of funding. The data suggests strong evidence of homophilia—i.e. women seek angel capital from women and men seek angel capital from men. The authors additionally recognise a degree of homophily in the distribution of angel financing, albeit to a limited extent. In essence, it seems that angel investors who are women tend to exhibit a greater inclination towards investing in female-led businesses, while male investors choose to allocate their angelic money towards male-led enterprises. However, it is important to note that the findings do not demonstrate consistent patterns over time. There is a lack of data supporting the notion that female entrepreneurs are required to relinquish a higher proportion of equity in return for venture capital compared to their male counterparts. In general, the findings of the authors are heavily influenced by the limited involvement of women in heavenly capital and their comparatively lower degree of activity in comparison with males. Certain scholars have drawn attention to the phenomenon known as the female discouragement effect in the context of securing financial resources. Capital is the main ingredient for growing a business and represents one of the most challenging problems of an entrepreneur (Carter et al. 2003; Neeley and Van Auken 2010); therefore, it can be useful to understand if there are gender biases. In this regard, the study by Eddleston et al. (2016) analyses the variability of the amount of the male and female loans, as it represents the most common source of external financing of women entrepreneurs according to Constantinidis et al. (2006). The analysis tool used by the authors is the theory of signals (Spence 1973) to be able to capture those signs of the entrepreneur's project feasibility and his commitment to the business, aspects that can explain differences in the loan amounts received by men and women. Signal theory has been repeatedly applied in the entrepreneurship literature to examine how investors evaluate the quality signals underlying their investment, including: business profitability and entrepreneur commitment, to evaluate the potential of entrepreneurial initiatives (Ozmel et al. 2013; Prasad et al. 2000), but the use of the theory is less widespread to consider how the meaning of the signals varies according to the type of the investor and, in particular, his sex theory (Eagly and Karau 2002) to verify how the gender of the investor impacts the gender of the recipient of funding. The study makes a valuable contribution to the existing body of literature by establishing a connection between gender roles and signalling theory. It effectively illustrates how the advantages derived from quality signals might differ based on the gender of the individual transmitting the signals. The research findings shed light on the differential remuneration of signs of feasibility and commitment exhibited by male and female entrepreneurs in comparison with capital providers. This discrepancy often results in a disadvantageous outcome for women. Consequently, the study reveals that the qualitative indicators influencing investment decisions are not consistently aligned with an equitable allocation of resources between genders. To clarify, the gender of the capital source has a detrimental effect on the issue of gender discrimination. The study's research closes by demonstrating the presence of biases against women entrepreneurs in relation to bank funding. Nevertheless, it appears that there is no substantial gender-based discrimination in the challenges associated with effectively expressing qualitative signals that underlie investment decisions. In other words, both men and women have similar difficulties in communication inside the banking front office.

The empirical literature provides different results regarding the gender disparity on bank loans compared to that which focuses on private equity and institutional capital, and like Eddleston et al. (2016) also Ongena and Popov (2015) tackle the problem of gender discrimination created by the supply of credit and the socio-economic system. The researchers conduct a survey of the immigrant community in the United States, focusing on inquiries on the societal role of women. From the collected replies, they derive an exogenous indicator of gender prejudice. The dataset pertains to approximately 6,000 small enterprises across 17 nations and demonstrates a connection between a pronounced gender bias and the deterrence of female entrepreneurs from seeking loans to fund their ventures. Consequently, these entrepreneurs opt for alternative sources of financing, such as informal channels, rather than abandoning their projects altogether. Additionally, the data does not appear to indicate discernible variations in risk profiles between female entrepreneurs and their male counterparts. This situation has greater validity in nations where there is a significant prevalence of gender-based bias towards women. Alesina et al. (2013) also bring attention to the issue where banks do not treat individuals with similar solvency risk profiles equally in terms of loan provision, based on their gender. The authors suggest that women, who are perceived as more risky, may face higher interest rates from banks, although they do not provide a concrete counterfactual to support this claim. There exists a disparity of around 28 basis points in the credit issued between individuals of different genders. Furthermore, when considering loan amounts of 60,000 euros, the yearly cost differential between men and women ranges from 55 to 170 euros. The dataset pertains to micro-enterprises in Italy, with a notable proportion of 25% being operated by female entrepreneurs. Hertz (2011) carries out a study in the United Kingdom, Europe, and America highlighting how women are discriminated against by banks as customers. During the 2008–2009 financial crisis, significant attention was directed towards subprime loans, governance structures, control mechanisms, and more. However, there was limited analysis regarding how banks have historically treated and continue to treat female customers. The research results highlight: evidence in the United Kingdom of banks, including prestigious and well-known banks in the credit market in which pregnant women and women on maternity leave in search of mortgages are sold and discriminated against, a very frequent aspect in the United Kingdom. Hertz anticipates the results of Alesina et al. (2013) by showing how in Europe banks discriminate against women entrepreneurs by highlighting the greater guarantees required of women who are charged higher rates than men for loans and are refused loans more frequently than men. The research also addresses the issue of gender stereotypes by bank loan officers internationally, providing some evidence in the United Kingdom. In particular, the findings of the contribution suggest those female entrepreneurs are asked to provide much more documentation about their business than male candidates, and among these, the target is pregnant women whom loan officers assume will not return to work afterwards, after having had a child. Last but not least, the research questions the training of loan officers. Muravyev et al. (2009) reach the same conclusions as Alesina and Hertz, using the cross-country Business Environment and Enterprise Performance Survey (BEEPS).

In the literature, it emerges that women are valued more by stereotypes than by their results, especially by banks, heavily influencing the budget constraint from which to start entrepreneurial activities. Buttner and Rosen's (1988) research verifies whether female entrepreneurs are also considered in terms of sexual stereotypes. The authors' findings are based on one hundred and six questioned bank loan officers who rated successful men, women, or entrepreneurs on scales that rated nine attributes of successful entrepreneurs. The nine entrepreneurial qualities evaluated by the respondents in the survey are: leadership, autonomy, risk appetite, willingness to change, resistance, lack of emotion, low need for support, low conformity, and persuasiveness. Women were shown to be perceived as inferior to males in terms of their likelihood of achieving entrepreneurial success across eight dimensions. However, it is worth noting that statistical significance was not achieved in relation to low conformism and persuasiveness. The authors postulate that the view of women's business success, in comparison with males, has been negatively influenced by gender and stereotypes as seen by loan officers. This study also closes by proposing government policies that advocate for the training of loan officers to address gender preconceptions. It also recommends the encouragement of women to enhance their communication skills in order to challenge conventional gender biases during loan application interviews.

2.3 The EU Initiatives Supporting Female Entrepreneurs

This section is a concise overview of current measures implemented by the European Union (EU) to facilitate and promote female entrepreneurship within small and medium-sized enterprises (SMEs). Notable examples include the Small Business Act and the Entrepreneurship 2020 Action

Plan. Among the most relevant policy measures at the international level that include policy against gender discrimination in the labour market, there is the Small Business Act (SBA), an initiative to help the people of Value Added Tax (VAT) and the small and medium-sized enterprises (SMEs) that represent the heart and the most important and consistent part of the Italian economy and, in general, of the European one. 99% of the companies of the Old Continent, in fact, belong to this category and that is why it constitutes the fundamental element for the employment growth and economic development of the whole of Europe. Fortunately, even in the eyes of the European Union the importance of small and medium-sized enterprises (SMEs) for the community economy has not gone unnoticed and proof of this SBA, a Communication of the European Commission of the 25 June 2008, later also approved by the Council and the European Parliament, which has developed a series of guiding principles and concrete actions to support the SMEs of the Union. The SBA, in fact, was created with the main objective of encouraging the growth, development, and competitiveness of European small and medium-sized enterprises and of making the possibility of doing business attractive and positive, through a series of facilitations that the Act suggests and proposes to undertake, at the administrative, legislative, and political level, to the various EU Member States. The SBA is part of the broader and more ambitious "Europe 2020" project, which includes, among its main objectives, the development of initiatives that stimulate economic growth in the European Union, such as a series of measures that can make the context in which companies operate more favourable and welcoming. The founding principle of the Small Business Act is the slogan "Think small first" or "Think small first", that is, to think first of all of the small and medium-sized enterprises, to break down the obstacles, mainly administrative and financial, that hinder their development. A principle that the European Commission invites us to keep in mind is both community policy and the national policy of the Member States. The ten points of the SBA, however, provide as many as 10 key principles, including the one mentioned above, which are intended to be a starting point and guide the political and legislative action of Europe and the states of the Union in favour of SMEs: create an environment in which entrepreneurs and family businesses can thrive and which is rewarding for the entrepreneurial spirit; ensure that honest entrepreneurs, who have experienced insolvency, quickly get a second chance; formulate rules in accordance with the "Think Small First" principle; make public administrations permeable to the needs of SMEs; adapt public intervention to the needs of SMEs; facilitate the participation of SMEs in public procurement and make better use of the possibilities of state aid for SMEs; facilitate the access of SMEs to credit and develop a legal and economic environment that favours the punctuality of payments in commercial transactions; help SMEs to benefit from the opportunities offered by the single market; promote the updating of skills in SMEs and all forms of innovation; enable SMEs to transform environmental challenges into opportunities; encourage and support SMEs to benefit from market growth. The European Commission's initiative aimed to establish a foundation for creating a conducive environment at both national and community levels to foster the growth and expansion of small businesses. This was to be achieved through measures such as simplifying regulations and administrative processes, facilitating access to financial resources, capitalising on the opportunities presented by the single market, and garnering support from the Public Administration. The primary objective of these initiatives is to foster the entrepreneurial mindset among Europeans, with a particular emphasis on facilitating the establishment of new enterprises and the growth of existing ones. This is made possible by the utilisation of the many benefits provided by both European Union regulations and domestic legislations. The Small Business Act and European legislation are two significant legal frameworks that have been established to support and regulate small businesses within the European Union. These legislative measures aim to provide a favourable environment for small businesses to thrive and contribute to economic growth and job creation. The Small Business Act, specifically designed for However, the Small Business Act goes beyond merely providing guidelines for the implementation of new laws, at both the community and individual Member State levels, in support of small and medium-sized enterprises (SMEs). It also includes a range of legislative proposals and concrete actions aimed at better addressing the specific needs of these businesses. For instance, it encompasses a general exemption regulation on state aid (EC Reg. no. 800/2008) that has already been approved. This regulation streamlines the process for granting aid to SMEs by public administrations. Additionally, there is a proposed regulation for a new Statute of the "European Private Company" that has not yet been implemented. This statute aims to provide Union entrepreneurs with a unified regulatory framework across European territories, facilitating the establishment of companies in different Member States. There are currently two directives on Value Added Tax (VAT) that have been adopted. Directive 2009/47/EC permits Member States to implement a reduced VAT rate for specific labour-intensive services. Another directive, which is still under discussion, aims to simplify and standardise the community rules on VAT invoicing. Additionally, an amendment to Directive 2000/35/EC on late payment is being considered to enhance its effectiveness. The "Erasmus for young entrepreneurs" initiative enables aspiring young business owners to gain entrepreneurial and linguistic skills by spending a designated period in companies located in other European countries. The European Investment Bank (EIB) will undertake measures to facilitate credit and financing accessibility for small and medium-sized enterprises (SMEs). Furthermore, an online e-business guide will be made available to SMEs, and a review of the Eco-Management and Audit Scheme (EMAS), a voluntary environmental management system, will be conducted to simplify its adoption by small and medium-sized enterprises. In 2011, the European Commission conducted a comprehensive assessment known as the "SBA Review" to evaluate the progress made in implementing the principles of the Small Business Act (SBA). The review revealed that a majority of the proposed initiatives, including legislative proposals (excluding the Statute of the European Private Company), had been adopted. However, it also highlighted the diverse approaches taken by individual Member States in implementing the SBA, resulting in varying outcomes, particularly in terms of alleviating administrative and bureaucratic burdens for small and medium-sized enterprises (SMEs). Additionally, based on the conducted analysis, the Commission has put forth additional measures to incorporate the Small Business Act into the "Europe 2020" strategy. These measures include the implementation of the "once only" principle, which allows small and medium-sized enterprises (SMEs) to request administrative documents and information only once. Furthermore, the Commission proposes to provide guarantees on financing for SMEs, enabling them to effectively address the challenges posed by the environment and globalisation. Additionally, efforts will be made to facilitate SMEs' access to the single European market and promote collaboration and aggregation among European companies. In 2014, a subsequent analysis of the Small Business Act was done, which acknowledged the advancements made so far. However, it also identified several challenges, namely pertaining to the acquisition of financial resources, the simplification of regulatory, administrative, and bureaucratic processes, and the facilitation of market access. In 2010, Italy approved the directive implementing the Small Business Act (SBA) as a response to the initiative of the European Commission. This directive mandated the continuous monitoring of policies aimed at supporting small and medium-sized enterprises (SMEs) and the development of an annual legislation specifically tailored for small businesses. Moreover, subsequent to the 2011 SBA Review, an initiative known as the "regionalisation of the SBA" was implemented. This initiative acknowledges the diverse economic and geographical disparities within Italy and aligns the Small Business Act with the distinct entrepreneurial landscapes throughout the Italian regions. The Italian Government has primarily prioritised productive investments, particularly in the areas of innovation, research and development, corporate finance modernisation, and the internationalisation of the production system, as part of their efforts to implement the Small Business Act (SBA). In order to support small and medium-sized enterprises (SMEs) across different sectors of development, the government has provided a range of subsidies. Nevertheless, it is primarily prosperous corporations that receive recognition, with assistance from the government, in their endeavours to expand globally, foster innovation, and adapt to the emerging issues brought about by globalisation.

Another initiative is the European Commission's Entrepreneurship 2020 Action Plan, which aims to revitalise entrepreneurship in Europe through various supportive measures over the period 2014–2020. It is based on three pillars: development of entrepreneurial education and training, creating a suitable business environment and contact with role models and specific groups so that entrepreneurship education and training create an environment where entrepreneurs can thrive and grow, developing role models, and reaching out to specific groups whose entrepreneurial potential is under-realised or unreachable through traditional business assistance.

The Entrepreneurship Action Plan is a decisive action blueprint to unlock European entrepreneurial potential, remove existing barriers, and revolutionise European entrepreneurial culture. Investing in changing public perceptions of entrepreneurship, educating about entrepreneurship, and supporting underrepresented groups among entrepreneurs are essential to bring about lasting change. Entrepreneurship in Europe will flourish in the long term only if many Europeans perceive an entrepreneurial career as a worthwhile and attractive option.

The Entrepreneurship 2020 Action Plan has been initiated by the European Commission with the aim of enhancing the entrepreneurial capacity of Europe. The generation of employment opportunities in Europe is mostly attributed to the establishment of new enterprises, particularly small and medium-sized enterprises (SMEs). However, it is worth noting that a significant proportion, around 50%, of these organisations face failure within the initial five-year period. Consequently, policymakers are actively engaged in implementing measures aimed at facilitating the success and expansion of entrepreneurial ventures. The strategy further implemented strategies to incentivise the establishment of start-ups and new enterprises, enhance the efficacy of corporate ownership transfers, and provide improved accessibility to financial resources. The proposal also seeks to create new bankruptcy regulations with the intention of facilitating the recovery of businesses following bankruptcy, since "second starters" have demonstrated a tendency towards success. According to a Eurobarometer study, the inclination of European citizens to engage in self-employment decreased from 45% to 37% due to the uncertainty that ensued following the financial and sovereign debt crises. This study was conducted as part of the objectives pursued by Eurobarometer, which collaborates with Member States, business organisations, and other relevant stakeholders to formulate roadmaps containing specific objectives and deadlines.

The availability of cash is crucial for the viability of a business, making it very challenging to continue one without such resources. Consequently, it is approximated that women-owned enterprises constitute slightly more than 30% of all legally registered firms on a global scale. However, it is observed that a significant proportion, namely 70%, of small and medium-sized enterprises (SMEs) run by women in developing nations face financial exclusion or have difficulties in obtaining financial services under fair conditions to fulfil their requirements. The aforementioned figure indicates that the yearly loan gap for small firms managed by women in formal sectors amounts to around $300 billion. The limited access to networks, expertise, and connections to high-quality marketplaces serves as an additional constraint on women's entrepreneurship. Women entrepreneurs have a crucial role in driving economic development by facilitating growth and generating employment opportunities, particularly for the most economically disadvantaged 40% of the population. Nevertheless, female entrepreneurs encounter several obstacles when it comes to securing funding, establishing ownership, and expanding their enterprises. These issues encompass restricted availability of finance and technology, insufficient access to networks and knowledge resources, as well as legal and political impediments that impede business ownership and growth. Women-led enterprises tend to have a higher concentration in retail and service industries, which are characterised by limited profitability and development prospects, while their presence in more lucrative sectors such as construction, electronics, and software remains relatively rare. The limited access to networks and information poses a constraint on women's entrepreneurial endeavours. According to empirical research, there is evidence to suggest that males tend to possess a greater number of social relationships compared to women. This disparity in social connections potentially affords men with enhanced access to various commercial prospects, information resources, and networking possibilities. This places women in an unfavourable position from the beginning. The scarcity of professional contacts, role models, and mentorship opportunities can have a detrimental impact on the business over an extended period of time.

In order to facilitate the empowerment of women entrepreneurs, the recently established Women Entrepreneurs Finance Initiative (We-Fi) aims to provide funding exceeding $1 billion. This funding will be utilised to enhance the accessibility of capital, offer technical support, and invest in initiatives and programmes that support small and medium-sizedenterprises (SMEs) led by women and girls in countries that are clients of the World Bank Group. The partners of We-Fi include of prominent Development Banks around the globe, including the World Bank (WB)-IFC, European Bank (EB), Asian Development Bank (ADB), African Development Bank Group (ADBG), Islamic Development Bank (IDB), and Inter-American Development Bank (IADB). The We-Fi programme aims to foster female entrepreneurship as a means to achieve gender balance and combat gender discrimination, therefore enhancing the likelihood of success. The objective of this initiative is to utilise donor funds to secure investments of up to $200 million and facilitate the mobilisation of $800 million or more in global financial and commercial financing. This will be achieved through collaboration with financial intermediaries, funds, and other market participants, potentially adopting similar approaches as the International Finance Corporation's (IFC) Women Entrepreneurs Opportunity Facility/Banking on Women programme. The We-Fi facility aims to address obstacles to financial access and provide additional services, such as capacity building, access to networks and mentors, and opportunities to connect with domestic and international markets. Its objective is to enhance the business environment for small and medium-sized enterprises (SMEs) owned or led by women in developing countries. The Women Entrepreneurs Finance Initiative (We-Fi) contributes to the realisation of both traditional and modern programmes of the World Bank Group and other partners. It expands its reach to new regions, supports the advancement of women-led enterprises in early stages of development, and enhances access to financial resources and protective services. Simultaneously, the objective of the initiative is to support supplementary measures in the public sector that strengthen the facilitating environment and enhance market opportunities for women entrepreneurs. We-Fi addresses the absence of substantial funding or organisations dedicated to a comprehensive public–private sector strategy for tackling the challenges encountered by women entrepreneurs. We-Fi provides dedicated resources to foster innovation and new approaches to removing these barriers for women entrepreneurs. It also helps to raise the issue and get governments and the private sector to take action. We-Fi is a Financial Intermediation Fund (FIF) owned by the World Bank and draws on the banks' strong track record of designing and managing such funds to ensure best practices in terms of governance and efficiency. The bank will act as trustee of the facility, leveraging its financial platform and extensive experience in providing such services to other of her FIFs. It also serves as the secretariat. Multilateral development banks, including the World Bank and IFC, are eligible implementation partners to propose private and public sector activities supported by the facility. Allocation decisions are made by a steering committee composed of the facility's founders.

2.4 G7 Initiatives

Policies have also been undertaken at the G7 level to combat gender discrimination in entrepreneurship and in the labour market in general and at an even wider level within society. The purpose of this initiative is to empower and enable women and girls globally to actively participate in and reap the benefits of gender equality efforts. In the context of pandemic recovery, it is crucial to consider the inclusion of those who have been marginalised based on factors like as race, ethnicity, age, disability, sexual orientation, gender identity, and socio-economic position. The GEAC 2021 conference builds upon the inaugural GEAC meeting during Canada's G7 leadership in 2018, as well as the subsequent GEAC gathering organised by the Office of the President of France in 2019. Elizabeth Truss, before to assuming the position of Prime Minister of the United Kingdom subsequent to Boris Johnson, served as a Member of Parliament and held the portfolio of Minister for Women and Equality. During her tenure, she endeavoured to uphold fundamental tenets such as freedom, equal opportunity for women, individual human rights, and the well-being of girls globally. In view of the ongoing recovery efforts from the COVID-19 pandemic, as emphasised by the Global Economic and Agricultural Challenges (GEAC) report of 2021, some pragmatic suggestions might be put up about the collaboration among the G7 nations. Promote the improvement of reconstruction efforts and guarantee equal opportunities for all individuals. To achieve success, it is imperative to prioritise both national and global initiatives. The UK Presidential Office has strategically aligned these elements with its priority gender equality concerns, which encompass education, empowerment, and the eradication of violence against women and girls. This alignment capitalises on the board of directors' robust scientific expertise in the fields of Science, Technology, Engineering, and Mathematics (STEM). A robust correlation exists among these three domains. Following deliberations on the topic of gender equality, Sarah Sands, together with her colleague Dr. Denis Mukwege, a Nobel Peace Prize laureate and member of the Gender Equality Advisory Council (GEAC), delivered the proposals formulated by the GEAC to the head of the G7:

1. Recognising the disproportionate effects of COVID-19 on Women and Girls Worldwide, Increasing Gender Transformation Development Programs, Sexual and Reproductive Health Services, and Addressing A "Shadow Pandemic" of Violence Against Women and Girls (VAWG).
2. Considering Pandemic Response and Recovery Understanding the needs of women and girls and monitoring their impact on Men's and Women's Recovery Initiatives, considering factors such as age, income, and disability ethnicity.
3. At least 12 years of transsexual education. All based on G7 Foreign and Development Minister's Efforts for Girls' Education and Family Support schools to implement gender-sensitive measures for the mental and physical health of girls.
4. A strengthened national and international community, access to care infrastructure and affordability quality care, including childcare, and increased public investment to address gender equality and imbalance between paid and unpaid care work.

5. Equal access to capital and labour markets; by removing barriers and creating employment opportunities and financing opportunities for women succeeding in Modern Business and Tailoring Guidelines for Supporting Female Owned micro and small and medium-sized enterprises (MSMEs).
6. Recognise the impact of global trade on women as merchants, workers, and consumers with G7 heads of state and governments in building trade ties benefiting women and girls around the world.
7. A gender-focused perspective on climate change encompassing financial, investment, and political dimensions. The 26th United Nations Climate Change Conference (COP 26) and the G7 heads of state and government have set objectives to provide resources towards girls' education, women's retraining, and lifelong learning. This initiative aims to guarantee that women and girls may effectively participate and reap the benefits of the ongoing "green" revolution.
8. Recognising risks to global prosperity women's economic empowerment, gender imbalance in STEM education, and a career and commitment that prioritise progress towards gender equality through concrete means.
9. Addressing the Digital Gender Gap support initiatives that help women, affordable, reliable, and secure Internet and mobile services to counteract algorithmic bias for women, girls, and marginalised groups disadvantage.
10. The end of stereotypes and inequality Treatment of women in the media, including support for the intergenerational equality forum commitment charter for culture and culture creative industry.
11. Global action to end violence against women and increased investment in girls' prevention and response; ratification of relevant conventions including Istanbul conventions; and improved support elimination of female genital mutilation (FGM).
12. Women and girls, Laws Imposing a Duty of Care Technology companies improving security for users online, including proper administration of pornographic sites on the Internet.
13. Condemnation of sexual violence used ways of war as an international red line, formulation of international treaties condemn, consistent with other prohibitions weapons of war such as mines chemical weapons.

14. Continuous action to monitor progress on gender equality and accountability commitments including the United Nations Sustainable Development Goals (SDGs), Establishment of the G7-GEAC Observatory Mechanism of measurement and reporting G7 progress.

Those just described represent a set of underlying recommendations or issues, including some corresponding educational measures for STEM girls and strengthening the international response to conflict-related sexual violence to promote a coherent and sustainable gender equality direction, through a commitment of all G7 and GEAC member countries. Nevertheless, it is important to note that efforts to address gender discrimination extend beyond the scope of the G7. The Organisation for Economic Co-operation and Development (OECD) also plays a significant role in this regard. The document titled "Gender Equality and Empowerment of Women and Girls: guidance for developing countries" offers valuable insights into the objectives set by the OECD to tackle gender discrimination, both in a broader context and specifically within the labour market. The objective of this handbook is to provide support to DAC Members and other development partners in their endeavours to promote and enhance gender equality. The policy, strategic planning, and leadership of the OECD Development Assistance Committee (DAC) may be utilised by its members to tackle issues related to gender equality and the empowerment of women and girls.

DAC members' political support for gender equality and the empowerment of women and girls are strong. The COVID-19 pandemic has had far-reaching socio-economic impacts, also demonstrating that all efforts to strengthen gender equality are essential for greener, gender-responsive, and sustainable construction (OECD 2018). Based on the most recent development cooperation policy of members belonging to the Development Assistance Committee (DAC), it is evident that 29 out of the total 30 countries have acknowledged the significance of gender equality and the empowerment of women and girls as a prominent political objective. Women have been actively participating in this domain for several decades and have only lately begun to cultivate strategies and resources to promote gender equality. Members of the Development Assistance Committee (DAC) actively incorporate gender views into their policies and strategies across several priority areas and sectors of development cooperation. The majority of DAC members have modified or restructured their policy approaches to address gender equality, using a dual strategy that involves both dedicated and integrated support for promoting gender equality.

It is considered advantageous for members of the DAC to employ a dual approach, wherein they integrate gender equality into their policies, plans, and programmes, while concurrently executing specific initiatives aimed at promoting gender equality and empowering women and girls. It is a DAC practice that expects member policies to recognise "the social, economic and environmental dimensions of sustainable development". Incorporating a dedication to policy consistency for the purpose of achieving sustainable development is deemed vital. This approach offers a coherent strategy for the alleviation of poverty, the mitigation of gender disparities, and the imperative of inclusivity. It is also expected to have specific guidance for integrating cross-cutting issues such as variability, conflict, and fragility. DAC validates these requirements using peer reviews. Members are expected to use the DAC Gender Equality Policy Markers when reporting Official Development Assistance (ODA) to the OECD. Furthermore, the OECD Recommendation on Gender Equality in Public Life encourages advocates to mainstream gender equality in the design, development, implementation, and evaluation of relevant public policies and budgets (OECD 2016, 2018). Certain DAC members consider gender equality as a legal need within the realm of international development. The integration of gender equality within the legislative framework of development cooperation has demonstrated its efficacy as a valuable mechanism for fostering motivation and ensuring responsibility. The integration of gender equality should be prioritised in development cooperation policies and strategies and should be specifically addressed through the implementation of dedicated gender equality policies, action plans, and instruments. DAC members should continue to promote gender equality and the empowerment of women and girls as policy priorities and integrate their efforts into strategic development cooperation policy frameworks. Where possible, this could be included in development cooperation legislation to ensure it is resilient to global challenges and changing political climates. This approach fosters a long-term, sustained focus on gender equality and the empowerment of women and girls, counters potential and temporary policy shifts, and advances gender equality.

Some DAC members have made gender equality a legal requirement for development cooperation. The United Kingdom's International

Development (Gender Equality) Act 2014 establishes obligations to consider the impact of gender equality in development cooperation and humanitarian aid when making spending decisions. Compliance with gender equality laws is the minimum compliance requirement for any humanitarian or development intervention and provides a framework for proportional and mandatory consideration of gender equality impacts. The legislation was complemented by additional accountability initiatives to implement the Department for International Development's (DFI's) strategic vision of gender equality. This includes senior staff dedicated to promoting gender equality across the organisation and the development of dashboards to report progress against goals. The Austrian Federal Law on Development Cooperation (2003) commits the Federal Government to a number of principles relating to development cooperation. It stipulates that the equality of women and men must be taken into account in all measures.

Looking at the United States, it is important to cite the Women Entrepreneurship and Economic Empowerment (WEEE) Act of 2018, which was enacted on January 9, 2019. The WEEE Act aims to target development assistance to micro, small, and medium-sized enterprises, especially women. The law also includes a section on the United States Agency for International Development's (USAID) Gender Equality Policy, which specifically outlines many of the policy's goals (for example) to reduce its harmful impacts and empower women and girls to exercise their rights. The law also calls for the integration of gender equality and women's empowerment throughout programme cycles in each sector of USAID, and requires that all policies, projects, and activities be informed by gender analysis. The WEEE Act's definition of "gender analysis" is consistent with USAID's Automated Directives System, "Integrating Gender Equality and Female Empowerment in USAID's Program Cycle". So, there is the need to comply with the gender analysis requirement, to provide the agency with a repository of gender analyses, to enable reporting to the United States Congress, and to facilitate the exchange of information and best practices on gender integration. For this purpose, USAID has developed an internal online database to aggregate and compile the gender analyses carried out and used by all missions across the agency. Spain's law on international development cooperation (23/1998) identified as priorities human rights, equality, and non-discrimination. In addition, Spain's law for equality between men and women (3/2007) includes an article linked to development cooperation, mentioning the Gender Strategy as the normative instrument for applying the law in development cooperation. This has been fundamental to advancing progress on integrating gender equality in all processes, from planning to management and evaluation. Italy's "General law on international development cooperation" (Law 125/2014) explicitly includes gender equality among the fundamental objectives of development cooperation (Article 1). The Three-Year Plan 2019/2021 for Cooperation Programs and Policy Orientation, provided for in Article 12, also confirms gender equality and the empowerment of women and girls as one of the prior ities of Italy's development cooperation system. DAC members also contribute to agenda-setting and policy-making on gender equality at the international and regional levels. It is good practice for DAC members to participate in the development of international standards and to be actively involved in promoting the inclusion of gender perspectives in global and regional discussions. These international and regional norms and standards guide the commitment of her DAC members to gender equality and the empowerment of women and girls, both domestically and in foreign policy and development cooperation. The Committee on the Elimination of Discrimination against Women (CEDAW) and the Beijing Declaration and Platform for Action are among the most prominent international legal and policy instruments focused on gender equality, recognising the link between development and gender equality. DAC members have been involved in setting standards for gender equality in development cooperation. Gender perspectives are also considered in other DAC legal documents. For example, 2019 DAC recommendations on the relationship between human development and peace [OECD/LEGAL/5019] contain several references to gender equality. Many DAC members recognise several reasons to work on gender equality and the empowerment of women and girls. They believe in the inherent value of gender equality and the empowerment of women and girls. Women around the world today have fewer opportunities, earn less, face more obstacles, and are subject to more violence and harassment than men. Gender equality is a fundamental human right. Members of the Development Assistance Committee (DAC) also acknowledge the potential of addressing gender inequality to enhance the competitiveness and sustainability of economies in partner countries, as well as to improve the efficacy and longevity of development cooperation efforts. However, it is important to note that this recognition may sometimes overshadow the importance of addressing human rights concerns. Some DAC members assert that the imperative to address gender equality in development stems from its status as a global concern necessitating collective action, while also aligning with the fundamental principles of their democratic systems. Over the past 15 years, DAC members' comprehensive policy focus on the empowerment of women and girls in gender equality and development has increased, including new DAC members. Most development cooperation is supervised by the foreign ministries or development cooperation departments of member countries. Some of these frameworks have taken the form of Action Plans for Gender Equality. Other DAC members have prioritised gender equality by adopting a feminist foreign policy perspective. Multiple intersecting elements have been highlighted as influential in fostering a heightened dedication to gender equality and the empowerment of women and girls. The 2030 Agenda, especially Sustainable Development Goal 5 (SDG5), is key to such commitments. Some members believe that the results of gender equality audits are drawing attention as part of the implementation of new or updated development policies, strategies, or action plans. Increased international and political interest and subsequently increased funding have been cited as other reasons.

In 2013, the Slovak Republic and the Czech Republic, the youngest members of the Development Assistance Committee (DAC) in Slovenia, demonstrated their dedication to promoting gender equality by joining the committee. These relatively young DAC members found the organisation's growing commitment to gender equality and the empowerment of women and girls. Among these new members' development agendas, mainstreaming gender equality is the most popular approach to promoting gender equality and the empowerment of women and girls. In recent years, however, some have included the targeted actions and reflections needed to foster further progress. Slovenia recalls that gender equality has always been a focal point of its foreign policy. More recently, however, withinside the "Development Co-operation and Humanitarian Aid Strategy of the Republic of Slovenia, 2030", gender equality has shifted from being a cross-reducing difficulty and end up a critical factor of its improvement cooperation method and fulfilment of the SDGs. Under this policy, gender equality isn't simplest recognised as a cross-reducing theme; however, thematic priorities that assist gender equality as a cease goal, such as "girls' financial empowerment", "making sure sexual and reproductive health" and "finishing violence towards girls and ladies", also are addressed. Slovenia's second "National Action Plan on Women, Peace, and Security (2018–2020)" incorporates expanded and focused moves to strengthen gender equality thru awareness-raising, training and training, and in addition integration of a gender angle in security-associated policies. Furthermore, it imposes additional accountability for ethical and gender-related perspectives among employees while overseas assignments. The Slovak Republic has acknowledged gender equality, particularly the empowerment of girls, as a significant issue in its "Medium-Term Strategy for Development Cooperation of the Slovak Republic for 2014–2018". However, there has been a significant institutional change in the prioritisation of gender equality in recent years. The "Medium-Term Strategy for Development Cooperation of the Slovak Republic (2019–2023)" prioritises SDG5, which aims to achieve gender equality and empower girls and women. These objectives are integrated throughout all projects and activities undertaken by SlovakAid. Nevertheless, the Slovak Republic has implemented specific initiatives aimed at enhancing the endeavours of institutions in promoting gender equality. An essential need for development cooperation projects is to explicitly articulate their contributions towards the promotion of gender equality and the achievement of Sustainable Development Goal 5 (SDG5). The aforementioned alteration has led to heightened endeavours in promoting equality by means of empowering strategies, including the establishment of secure and equitable prospects in areas such as public life, education, health care, and economic engagement. In partnership with the United Nations Development Programme (UNDP), a guidebook on gender equality in development cooperation was prepared as a component of this endeavour. Intended for both donors and applicants, it will be released in September 2021, followed by a webinar.

The Czech Republic is also actively integrating gender equality and the empowerment of women and girls into its development cooperation policies and plans. The 2012 Czech Development Cooperation Report emphasises strategic initiatives that specifically prioritise the advancement of women and girls, with the aim of fostering their empowerment. In the Development Cooperation Strategy 2010–2017, "Respect for Fundamental Human, Economic, Social and Labor Rights" is one of three cross-cutting themes. This cross-cutting theme identifies efforts to mainstream gender equality and empowerment efforts across the programme, but gender equality is not explicitly highlighted as a cross-cutting theme. However, in the "Czech Republic Development Cooperation Strategy 2018–2030", "gender equality and the empowerment of women and girls" is a cross-cutting priority throughout the strategy. South Korea joined the DAC in 2010. South Korea's Medium-Term Gender Equality Strategy (2016–2020 and 2021–2025) aims to achieve SDG5 through two approaches, with gender equality as a goal in itself and cross-cutting themes rooted in all development programmes. In addition, Korea's International Cooperation Agency is leading a multi-stakeholder partnership to accelerate the achievement of SDG5 by addressing the root causes of gender inequality and ameliorating its impact ("SDG5 Fill the GAP"). Knowledge-sharing forums and events are also part of this initiative.

Examples of thematic priorities for gender equality are set to address key barriers to the empowerment of women and girls in areas where progress is usually slow or set back. With a long-term focus on gender equality, some of her established DAC members are able to advance gender equality across a range of thematic priorities. However, for smaller and newer members of the DAC, identifying their relative strengths and picking out a limited number of areas to focus more on gender equality and the empowerment of women and girls, assistance may be more beneficial. DAC members should consider comparative advantages and opportunities when defining thematic priorities for gender equality policy, and focus on thematic areas where progress is slow or declining. There are many priority areas that need to be addressed when addressing gender equality and the empowerment of women and girls.

For this purpose, women's economic empowerment DAC members' focus on women's economic empowerment in development cooperation is a critical response to rising poverty rates and the feminisation of poverty. Women's economic empowerment is often a prerequisite for other gender equality goals, such as women's empowerment, sexual and reproductive health and rights, and ending gender-based violence. Women's economic empowerment has the potential to create a more competitive and sustainable economy. If women participated in the economy at the same rate as men, it is estimated that in 2025 she would add $28 trillion, or 26% of the annual global GDP, compared to the normal scenario (McKinsey Global Institute 2015). There is no single definition of women's economic empowerment, and the scope of women's economic empowerment is so wide that most members also address several sub-themes of this priority theme in their policies and the most common of these is "entrepreneurship", decent work, resource access and management, private sector and business governance, agriculture, and rural development. A subset of countries within the Development Assistance Committee (DAC) have implemented alternative strategies, action plans, or recommendations that are specifically designed to tackle the issue of women's economic empowerment (OECD 2022a, b, c). Several DAC members perceive the Decent Work Agenda, encompassing elements such as job generation, labour rights, social security, and social discourse, as an essential component of efforts aimed at promoting women's economic empowerment. In terms of gender equality, numerous DAC members acknowledge the significance of addressing the issue of unpaid care work as a significant obstacle to women's economic empowerment, particularly within the context of the COVID-19 pandemic. To develop women's monetary empowerment via thematic prioritisation, DAC individuals can align with the seven key "drivers for transformation" diagnosed with the aid of using the UN Secretary-General's High-Level Panel on Women's Economic Empowerment (UN Women 2017). These drivers are: tackling detrimental norms and selling fantastic function models; ensuring felony safety and reforming discriminatory legal guidelines and regulations; recognising, lowering, and redistributing unpaid paintings and care; building assets—digital, monetary, and property; changing enterprise lifestyle and practice; improving public area practices in employment and procurement; strengthening visibility, collective voice, and representation. DAC individuals' bilateral useful resource to the monetary and efficient sectors that combine gender equality is regularly increasing (OECD 2021). However, a contrast between the financing of sub-issues of monetary empowerment and political commitments to those sub-issues suggests combined results. For example, the improved cooperation and gender equality regulations of many DAC individuals point out banking and enterprise as a thematic priority; however, the full-size scope stays to grow their investments in gender equality in those sectors.

Ending gender-based violence and fragility, women, peace and security, and humanitarian assistance are other priorities of DAC members for gender equality policy that we don't discuss in this section, to focus on economic aspects of gender inequality.

In summary, several worldwide efforts have been established to address gender disparity, encompassing not only the most developed countries, such as the G7. Despite this, there are not many initiatives to combat the phenomenon credit disparities within the banking sector. This aspect requests further examination by countries in order to foster more equitable economic growth. Numerous studies have shown that addressing this factor can lead to more inclusive economic development, as opposed to an economy that primarily benefits a select few individuals. In relation to this matter, the International Finance Corporation (IFC) and the World Bank are putting out measures, although there is limited national-level action to address the situation. Policymakers in any nation has the authority to disseminate initiatives on a worldwide scale, and it is imperative that more action be taken in this area.

References

Agier, I., and Szafarz, A. (2013). Microfinance and gender: Is there a glass ceiling on loan size? *World Development*, *42*, 165–181.

Ahl, H. (2006). Why research on women entrepreneurs needs new directions. *Entrepreneurship Theory and Practice*, *30*(5), 595–621.

Alesina, A. F., Lotti, F., and Mistrulli, P. E. (2013). Do women pay more for credit? Evidence from Italy. *Journal of the European Economic Association*, *11*(1), 45–66.

Becker-Blease, J. R., and Sohl, J. E. (2007). Do women-owned businesses have equal access to angel capital? *Journal of Business Venturing*, *22*(4), 503–521.

Bigelow, C. A., Pereira, G. A., Warmsley, A., Cohen, J., Getrajdman, C., Moshier, E., and Stone, J. (2014a). Risk factors for new-onset late postpartum preeclampsia in women without a history of preeclampsia. *American Journal of Obstetrics and Gynecology*, *210*(4), 338-e1.

Bigelow, L., Lundmark, L., McLean Parks, J., and Wuebker, R. (2014b). Skirting the issues: Experimental evidence of gender bias in IPO prospectus evaluations. *Journal of Management*, *40*(6), 1732–1759.

Bird, B., and Brush, C. (2002). A gendered perspective on organizational creation. *Entrepreneurship Theory and Practice*, *26*(3), 41–65.

Buttner, E. H., and Rosen, B. (1988). Bank loan officers' perceptions of the characteristics of men, women, and successful entrepreneurs. *Journal of Business Venturing*, *3*(3), 249–258.

Carter, N. M., Gartner, W. B., Shaver, K. G., and Gatewood, E. J. (2003). The career reasons of nascent entrepreneurs. *Journal of Business Venturing*, *18*(1), 13–39.

Carter, S., and Rosa, P. (1998). Indigenous rural firms: Farm enterprises in the UK. *International Small Business Journal*, *16*(4), 15–27.

Coleman S. (2000). Access to capital and terms of credit: A comparison of men–and women–owned small businesses. *Journal of Small Business Management, 38*(3), 37–52.

Coleman, S., and Robb, A. (2009), A comparison of new firm financing by gender: Evidence from the Kauffman Firm Survey data. *Small Business Economics, 33*, 397–411. https://doi.org/10.1007/s11187-009-9205-7.

Connell, R. W. (1990). An iron man: The body and some contradictions of hegemonic masculinity. In M. Messner, and D. Sabo (Eds.), *Sport, men and the gender order*. Champaign, IL: Human Kinetics Books.

Connell, R. W., and Messerschmidt, J. W. (2005). Hegemonic masculinity: Rethinking the concept. *Gender & Society*, *19*(6), 829–859.

Constantinidis, C., Cornet, A., and Asandei, S. (2006). Financing of women-owned ventures: The impact of gender and other owner-and firm-related variables. *Venture Capital*, *8*(02), 133–157.

Du Rietz, A., and Henrekson, M. (2000). Testing the female underperformance hypothesis. *Small Business Economics*, *14*, 1–10.

Eagly, A. H. (1987). *Sex differences in social behavior: A social-role interpretation*. Hillsdale, NJ: Lawrence Erlbaum.

Eagly, A. H., and Carli, L. L. (2003). The female leadership advantage: An evaluation of the evidence. *The Leadership Quarterly*, *14*(6), 807–834.

Eagly, A. H., and Karau, S. J. (2002). Role congruity theory of prejudice toward female leaders. *Psychological review*, *109*(3), 573.

Eddleston, K. A., Ladge, J. J., Mitteness, C., and Balachandra, L. (2016). Do you see what I see? Signaling effects of gender and firm characteristics on financing entrepreneurial ventures. *Entrepreneurship Theory and Practice*, *40*(3), 489–514.

Fabowale, L., Orser, B., and Riding, A. (1995). Gender, structural factors, and credit terms between Canadian small businesses and financial institutions. *Entrepreneurship Theory and Practice*, *19*(4), 41–65.

Fay, M., and Williams, L. (1993). Gender bias and the availability of business loans. *Journal of Business Venturing*, *8*(4), 363–376.

Freear, J., and Wetzel Jr, W. E. (1992). The informal venture capital market in the 1990s. In D. L. Sexton and J. D. Kasarda (Eds.), *State of the art of entrepreneurship* (pp. 462–486). Boston, MA: PWS-Kent.

Haines Jr, G. H., Orser, B. J., and Riding, A. L. (1999). Myths and realities: An empirical study of banks and the gender of small business clients. *Canadian Journal of Administrative Sciences/Revue Canadienne des Sciences de l'Administration*, *16*(4), 291–307.

Hertz, N. (2011). *Women and banks: Are female customers facing discrimination?* London: Institute for Public Policy Research. Available online at https://www.ippr.org/files/images/media/files/publication/2011/11/womenbanks_Nov2011_8186.pdf.

Hisrich, R., and Brush, C. (1984). *The woman entrepreneur: Management skills and business problems*. University of Illinois at Urbana-Champaign's Academy for Entrepreneurial Leadership Historical Research Reference in Entrepreneurship.

International Finance Corporation (2021, December). *IFC Annual Report 2021*. World Bank Publications - Books, The World Bank Group, number 36334.

Kalleberg, A. L., and Leicht, K. T. (1991). Gender and organizational performance: Determinants of small business survival and success. *Academy of Management Journal*, *34*(1), 136–161.

López-Zafra, E., Garcia-Retamero, R., and Eagly, A. H. (2009). Congruenza del ruolo di genere e aspirazioni delle donne a posizioni di leadership. *Giornale di psicologia sociale* , *24*(1), 99–108.

McKechnie, S. A., Ennew, C. T., and Read, L. H. (1998). The nature of the banking relationship: A comparison of the experiences of male and female small business owner. *International Small Business Journal*, *16*(3), 39–55.

McKinsey & Company (2015). *The power of parity: How advancing women's equality can add $12 trillion to global growth*, September. Available at: https://www.mckinsey.com/featured-insights/employment-and-growth/how-advancing-womens-equality-can-add-12-trillion-to-global-growth.

Muravyev, A., Talavera, O., and Schäfer, D. (2009). Entrepreneurs' gender and financial constraints: Evidence from international data. *Journal of Comparative Economics*, *37*(2), 270–286.

Neeley, L., and Van Auken, H. (2010). Differences between female and male entrepreneurs' use of bootstrap financing. *Journal of Developmental Entrepreneurship*, *15*(01), 19–34.

OECD (2016). *Entrepreneurship at a Glance*. Paris: OECD Publishing.

OECD (2018). *OECD toolkit for mainstreaming and implementing gender equality: Implementing the 2015 OECD recommendation on gender equality in public life*. https://www.oecd.org/gender/governance/toolkit/toolkit-for-mainstreaming-and-implementinggender-equality.pdf.

OECD (2021). *Development finance for gender equality and women's empowerment: A 2021 snapshot*. OECD DAC network on gender equality (gendernet). Available at: https://www.oecd.org/development/gender-development/Development-finance-for-gender-equality-2021.pdf.

OECD (2022a). *G7 dashboard on gender gaps – Germany*. Paris: OECD Publishing. https://www.g7germany.de/resource/blob/974430/2058072/5eafec9454770407b4f5719778ff7f50/2022-06-28-gender-gap-germany-data.pdf?download=1

OECD (2022b). *G7 dashboard on gender gaps – Italy*. Paris: OECD Publishing. https://www.g7germany.de/resource/blob/974430/2058170/3f90a9cb877a250f56245ede5adbf53a/2022-06-28-gender-gap-italy-data.pdf?download=1

OECD (2022c). *G7 dashboard on gender gaps – USA*. Paris: OECD Publishing. www.bmfsfj.de/resource/blob/199066/66728e8bae6287b5e8b2848d41fe53a6/g7-dashboard-on-gender-gaps-usa-data.pdf.

Ongena, S., and Popov, A. (2015). *Gender bias and credit access*. ECB Working Paper Series, no. 1822, July 2015.

Ozmel, U., Reuer, J. J., and Gulati, R. (2013). Signals across multiple networks: How venture capital and alliance networks affect interorganizational collaboration. *Academy of Management Journal*, *56*(3), 852–866.

Prasad, D., Bruton, G. D., and Vozikis, G. (2000). Signaling value to business angels: The proportion of the entrepreneur's net worth invested in a new venture as a decision signal. *Venture Capital: An International Journal of Entrepreneurial Finance*, *2*(3), 167–182.

Rosa, P., and Hamilton, D. (1994). Gender and ownership in UK small firms. *Entrepreneurship Theory and Practice*, *18*(3), 11–27.

Rosa, P., Carter, S., and Hamilton, D. (1996). Gender as a determinant of small business performance: Insights from a British study. *Small Business Economics*, *8*(6), 463–478. http://www.jstor.org/stable/40228670.

Schein, V. E., and Davidson, M. J. (1993). Think Manager, Think Male. *Management Development Review*, *6*(3). https://doi.org/10.1108/EUM0000000000738.

Spence, M. (1973, August). Job market signaling. *The Quarterly Journal of Economics*, *87*(3), 355–374. https://doi.org/10.2307/1882010.

UN Women (2017). *Annual report 2016–2017*. Available at: annualreport.unwomen.org

CHAPTER 3

Women in Alternative Finance: A Focus on the Equity Crowdfunding

Francesca Battaglia and Emanuela Giusi Gaeta

Abstract This chapter covers an examination of the fundamental attributes of crowdsourcing, with a specific emphasis on the operational procedures of equity crowdfunding. Afterwards, our focus shifts towards, examining the characteristics that may play a role in addressing the gender disparity evident in traditional financing channels, as well as distinguishing crowdfunding from other types of venture capital. The existing literature demonstrates that there is significant interest from scholars, policymakers, and practitioners in exploring the connection between female entrepreneurship and crowdfunding. Building upon this, the second part of this chapter aims to present an extensive examination of recent scholarly articles pertaining to this subject matter. This review will primarily concentrate on the outcomes of these studies and will also provide an analysis of the different competing theories.

This work reflects the author's opinions without engaging the Ministry's responsibility. The views expressed in the chapter are those of the author and do not involve the responsibility of the institutions to which she belongs.

F. Battaglia and E. Giusi Gaeta, *Women in Alternative Finance*,
https://doi.org/10.1007/978-3-031-43467-9_3

Keywords Crowdfunding · Women in the equity crowdfunding · Entrepreneurial efficiency and women' managerial management · EU regulation · Venture capital decision-making process · Managerial efficiencies

3.1 Crowdfunding Overview

In this section, we will examine the key features of crowdfunding, with a specific emphasis on its operational procedures. Next, we get into a more comprehensive analysis of the equity crowdfunding landscape.

Numerous definitions have been put up in response to the widespread adoption and prominence of crowdfunding. However, despite growing academic interest in crowdfunding, a thorough description that fully captures the complexities of this phenomenon remains elusive. Steinberg (2012) defines crowdfunding as an emphasis on public donations to raise funds for new ventures. However, the aforementioned definition neglects other factors, notably the influence of the Internet. Even Rubinton's (2011) definition does not cover the importance of social media and the Internet. Wicks (2013) places significant emphasis on the principles of fairness, contributions, and incentives. Similarly, Massolution (2012) ignores the role of the Internet and social networks, and of reward-based crowdfunding such as: B. Pre-Purchase. Harrington (2014), on the other hand, includes the role of the Internet in his definition, but the typical purpose of crowdfunding fundraising is unclear. Hemer's (2011) definition considers giving in exchange for a reward but does not cover other risky forms of crowdfunding, such as Equity Crowdfunding. Even the definition of Belleflamme et al. (2013) does not consider certain aspects such as: B. Peer-to-peer lending and financing by individuals or groups in fields such as music. Hemer's (2011) definition also does not cover peer-to-peer lending or equity capital aspects. Mollick (2014), on the other hand, tries to avoid the same trap by providing a definition that includes some additional elements of the crowdfunding phenomenon. De Buysere et al. (2012) also attempted to find a broader definition but did not emphasise the role of social networks, despite being an important part of the overall crowdfunding process. Moreover, while its definition ties in with the entrepreneurial perspective, the real purpose of crowdfunding goes far beyond that. It also ignores some prominent factors such as peer-to-peer lending. Lebraty and Lobre-Lebraty (2013) provide a simple definition but fail to articulate some basic elements of crowdfunding. Belt et al. (2012) consider most elements of crowdfunding, but lack lender expectations. In contrast to many other approaches, the definitions of Ingram and Teigland (2013) and Marom et al. (2016) give social networking its due importance.

If we want to give a more technical definition, we can see crowdfunding as a fundraising tool that aims to seek supporters for the financing of projects based not so much on the search for large capital, but rather on the contribution of small and medium-sized donors and financiers, generally through a digital platform. Find out everything there is to know about crowdfunding and the opportunities it offers to your organisation. What is crowdfunding? Crowdfunding (from crowd and funding financing) can be defined as a bottom-up involvement process, which reaches people interested in supporting other people's projects or non-profit organisations with their own money through an Internet platform. It is a fundraising tool that, although it has clearly "analogical" European historical experiences, it can be said that since the early 1900s it has developed mostly from the United States. In Italy, it was, in fact, launched for the first time in 2005 with the launch of the "Productions from the bottom" platform and has then exploded over the last few years. As of the year 2018, a total of 78 platforms of diverse kind have been identified.

3.1.1 *Types of Crowdfunding*

The crowdfunding world has developed in the last decade offering a varied and structured landscape and is not limited to fundraising only, but also includes financial activities. There are different types of crowdfunding fundraising activation that can be grouped as follows:

- *All or Nothing* (AON), in the event that the campaign objective is not met or surpassed within a 90-day timeframe, the entirety of the contributions will be refunded. This model is suitable for initiatives that require a minimum level of attainment in order to proceed with implementation;
- *Keep it all (KIA)*, all contributions collected in a maximum of 90 days are credited even if the campaign goal is not achieved. Aimed at projects that can start even if the amount foreseen by the objective has not been collected. The fundraising platform enables

individuals to engage in fundraising activities by providing immediate credit access, without imposing any predetermined minimum target or temporal constraints. This funding option is particularly well-suited for organisations, political parties, and public entities seeking to secure financial resources for sustaining their continuous operations.

The platforms can be divided also into:

- *donation/reward based*: the model with donation provides that those who donate money to the campaign do so in the form of a donation for causes that are close to their heart, without any kind of return, if not a thank you. The reward model, or rather with reward, remains within the scope of the donation, therefore of fundraising, but provides for a system of rewards, not financial, but proportionate, more or less symbolic, depending on the amount of the donation and linked to the cause.
- *loan-based*: it is a crowdfunding model represented by the loan of money, where a subject gives money as a loan, which therefore provides for the repayment of the sum. The amount of interest is possible and varies according to the methods chosen and the relationship with socially relevant causes or not.
- *Equity based*: consists of crowdfunding with investment. It is in fact an investment in shares or shares of companies, often start-ups, where a person buys shares of capital to have an economic return in relation to and according to the financing operation carried out. This kind of crowdfunding is in fact a solicitation of public savings and involves relative risks. Therefore, it is governed by specific rules in different countries: in Italy, the competent body is the National Commission for Companies and the Stock Exchange (CONSOB), which has issued a regulation since 2013.
- *DIY (Do it Yourself)*: these are personalised campaigns developed on independent sites in line with the identity of the project.

By focusing on equity crowdfunding, we can say that this is essentially a relatively new fundraising method: it was regulated in Italy in 2013. Italy turned out to be the first country in Europe (and substantially in the world, because in the USA already existed but with strong limitations) to introduce this type of legislation with a law and a subsequent regulation. Initially, however, equity crowdfunding did not take off also due to rules considered restrictive by the players in the sector. Subsequently, the regulation was amended several times, with a consequent boost to investments. The market is currently continuing to grow. As of 30 June 2018, the aggregate value of equity crowdfunding amounted to 33.3 million euros, with a specific sum of 20.9 million euros collected alone over the last year. This figure represents a notable increase of almost thrice compared to the preceding year.

Now, let us proceed to comprehend its functioning. Investing in firms via equity crowdfunding entails directing attention towards organisations that are perceived to possess the capacity for growth and market establishment. Capital is exchanged for monetary investment, resulting in a partnership formation. In the event of a firm in which an individual has made an investment achieving success, the shares owned by such individual will exhibit an increased value relative to the initial purchase price. Consequently, the individual may opt to realise a profit by selling these shares, or alternatively, they may elect to receive dividends. Conversely, in the event of a failed endeavour, which is a common occurrence for several businesses, there exists the potential for a whole or partial loss of the invested capital. It is important to bear in mind that this investment carries a significant level of risk.

The phenomenon of equity crowdfunding in Italy has exhibited a noteworthy trend over the course of many years. From 1 January to 2 December 2021, a total of 1,348 million euros were allocated to investments in start-ups and innovative enterprises in Italy. This figure represents a significant increase of 85% when compared to the corresponding period in 2020. The aforementioned statement is derived from the "Startup & Technology Trends" Report, which was curated by StartupItalia in conjunction with UpBase. In 2020, equity crowdfunding experienced the repercussions of the prevailing uncertainty caused by the pandemic. Particularly, during the middle of the year, the sector faced challenges. However, it also achieved commendable outcomes, primarily attributed to a substantial surge in offerings within the real estate market (known as real estate crowdfunding) and investment vehicles. Real estate platforms have garnered significant attention from investors due to their potential for secure and immediate profits. According to a study by cro wdfundingbuzz.it, the total amount raised in 2020 reached 103 million euros, which represents a significant increase of 57% compared to the 65 million euros raised in 2019. The expansion of financed campaigns had a somewhat lower degree of verticality in comparison with that of the collection, with a growth rate of 159 campaigns in contrast to 139 campaigns in 2019, or a 14% increase. As a result, there has been a significant rise in the average collecting amount for each campaign, with figures rising from 472 thousand euros to 648 thousand euros. One possible contributing factor to the exceptional collection performance in the previous quarter may be attributed to the expiration of the 50% tax incentive on December 31. In 2020, the expansion of equity crowdfunding was bolstered by investment vehicles, namely holding corporations that primarily engage in start-ups and innovative small and medium-sized enterprises (SMEs). The figures indicate a notable increase, with a total contribution of 23.7 million in 2020 compared to 3.5 million in the preceding year of 2019. The real estate crowdfunding sector has demonstrated positive outcomes, particularly for the emerging players, as seen by an almost twofold increase in capital raised compared to the previous year. Specifically, the amount collected rose from 16.5 million to 29.3 million, accompanied by an average collection size that grew from 1.1 million to 1.5 million. The assemblage of small and medium-sized enterprises (SMEs) and start-ups has a very modest trajectory of growth, with an increase from 45.5 million in 2019 to 50 million in 2020, or a 10% expansion. A total of 128 enterprises received financial backing, representing an increase over the 119 companies that were sponsored in the previous year of 2019. The mean collection is rather stable, with a recorded value of 391 thousand euros in 2020 and 383 thousand euros in 2019. Nevertheless, the pinnacle was attained in 2019 when equity crowdfunding exhibited remarkable performance, prompting discussions about a record-breaking year. The nine most active platforms in the country collectively raised over 65 million euros, nearly doubling the figures from 2018, which stood at 36 million euros. The quantity of financially supported campaigns has exhibited an upward trend, increasing from 113 in the year 2018 to 138 in the subsequent year of 2019, reflecting a growth rate of 18%. According to the surveys of Starteed (technology for crowdfunding), the best equity crowdfunding platforms of 2020 in terms of collection volumes were:

- Opstart: €22,800,870
- Crowdfundme: 17,540,000
- Walliance: €14,329,053
- Mamacrowd: 14,058,538
- Backtowork24: €13,533,963

The interaction between equity crowdfunding and small and medium-sized enterprises (SMEs) is a crucial element to consider. Since January of the previous year, equity crowdfunding has witnessed a significant development by expanding the market to encompass all small and medium-sized enterprises (SMEs), rather than just focusing on start-ups and innovative SMEs. Originally, the legislation stipulated that this method of fundraising was exclusively intended for start-up companies. However, as time has passed, there has been a growing demand to expand its application to innovative small and medium-sized enterprises (SMEs), which were initially included under a regulation enacted in 2015, and subsequently to all SMEs. In Italy, the number of small and medium-sized organisations (SMEs), defined as companies with less than 250 workers, amounts to around 760 thousand, accounting for 76% of the overall number of enterprises, which is equivalent to 996 thousand. These SMEs have an average annual growth rate of 5.6%, as reported by Data Market-Watch PMI and Banc Ifis Business. The audience of equity crowdfunding investors is therefore potentially very large. But what does the legislation say at the Italian and European levels?

The potential size of the audience for equity crowdfunding investors is considerable. However, it is important to examine the legislative provisions at both the Italian and European levels. Italy holds the distinction of being the first nation to establish regulations pertaining to the provision of risk financing for pioneering start-ups. Subsequently, this opportunity was expanded to encompass small and medium-sized enterprises (SMEs) that do not necessarily operate within the realm of innovation. The potentiality has materialised and has been officially implemented by the enactment of Legislative Decree 50/2017. The regulation and the Italian legislative framework date back to 2013, with 25 articles contained in the "Raising of venture capital by innovative companies and start-ups through online portals". This is a set of rules issued by the CONSOB, "daughters" of the "Growth decree bis", Legislative Decree 179/2012. In 2016, the USA opened equity crowdfunding to the entire "crowd" and not just to accredited investors (those who earn at least $200,000 a year or have available assets of at least $1 million). The innovative method of financing has been successful.

Thus far, the variations in national rules have posed obstacles to the facilitation of cross-border crowdfunding services. The fragmented legal framework across European borders has resulted in substantial legal expenses for platforms and individuals seeking capital. They frequently encounter challenges in identifying the applicable regulations for cross-border crowdfunding services or those offered in another Member State. Consequently, investors are typically dissuaded from engaging in cross-border investments via crowdfunding sites. Crowdfunding service providers are advised against extending their services to Member States where they are not established, due to similar rationales. In order to address the aforementioned challenges and achieve regulatory consistency, the "Regulation (EU) 2020/1503 of the European Parliament and of the Council of 7 October 2020 on European providers of crowdfunding services for businesses" was promulgated. The present document aims to revise the provisions of Regulation (EU) 2017/1129 and Directive (EU) 2019/1937. The European Union has made the decision to introduce a provision that allows equity and loan crowdfunding platforms to receive a European passport. This passport will enable these platforms to seek public savings and provide financial support to firms across all member nations of the European Union. The EU Regulation 2020/1503 pertaining to European crowdfunding service providers for enterprises becomes effective on 10 November 2021. Essentially, this framework facilitates the alignment of rules across different jurisdictions, hence promoting cross-border investments and funding. Regrettably, the appointment of the competent entity responsible for defining the technical standards necessary for the implementation of the European law in Italy has not yet been accomplished. What are the changes triggered by the new European Union Regulation? Establishing a unified regulatory framework for crowdfunding services in Europe is intended to facilitate the seamless operation of the whole sector within the European Union. The regulation stipulates that all countries within the European Union are entitled to equal provisions concerning online capital raising, with a maximum limit of 5 million euros. It emphasises the importance of service providers adopting a more professional, clear, and transparent approach to safeguard investors against potential losses. Additionally, the regulation calls upon each nation to establish procedures for authorising and overseeing crowdfunding providers. The objective is to streamline the disparate regulations governing crowdfunding in Europe, since each nation has independently enacted its own legislation for a considerable period of time. The newly implemented regulation requires that crowdfunding platforms have the opportunity to acquire a European passport from the relevant authority in their respective Member State. This passport grants them the authorisation to conduct operations in all Member States where they want to engage in their activities. Likewise, corporations will also get the opportunity to secure investments not alone within Italy, but across the entirety of the European Union. The regulatory framework also includes a range of stringent measures aimed at safeguarding investor interests and establishing standardised formats for the presentation of prospective business ventures.

The EU regulation aims to achieve the objectives of safeguarding savers and promoting openness. In order to uphold investor protection, mitigate crowdfunding risks, and promote equitable treatment of all clientele, it is imperative for crowdfunding service providers to establish a policy that guarantees the professional, unbiased, and transparent selection of projects on their platforms. An illustrative instance is the implementation of an entry examination to ascertain proficiency and simulate the capacity to endure financial setbacks (as per Article 21). This examination necessitates that the crowdfunding service provider evaluates the suitability of its offered services, specifically identifying those that are acceptable for prospective investors. Consequently, it is important to solicit details pertaining to one's prior experience, investing objectives, financial circumstances, and fundamental comprehension of the dangers inherent in investments as a whole. The regulation mandates the implementation of a "entrance test" to assess the unsophisticated investor's capacity to withstand losses, equivalent to 10% of their net assets. This test also serves to trigger an alert when specific parameters regarding the investment-to-equity ratio are surpassed. What possible scenarios for equity crowdfunding? Will this complex but inevitable change then lead the Italian equity and lending crowdfunding platforms to launch consolidation transactions (mergers/M&A) between operators in the sector? Or to evaluate the expansion from one sector to another, to create innovative synergies in a context in which none of the Italian platforms, to date, has ever allowed both the raising of equity capital and financing? To assess the transition from one industry to another with the aim of generating novel synergies, within a framework where none of the existing Italian platforms have facilitated both equity capital raising and finance thus far.

Predicting the trajectory of a dynamic and always increasing sector is a challenging task. However, there is a prevailing opinion that the crowdfunding industry has regressed to a state reminiscent of its nascent stage, nearly a decade ago.

3.2 Specific Features of the Equity Crowdfunding

This section is devoted to examining distinct characteristics of crowdfunding that differentiate it from other forms of venture finance, such as venture capital. In venture capital, entrepreneurs engage with extensively trained professional investors over an extended period of time to negotiate an equity agreement (Petty and Gruber 2011). In particular, we analyse those feature that potentially could contribute to bridge the gender gap observed in the other conventional funding markets. In this regard, we highlight that individuals who participate in crowdfunding campaigns face challenges related to the availability of trustworthy and verifiable information (Belleflamme et al. 2014; Moss et al. 2015). Additionally, they often lack direct communication with the creators of the projects they support (Courtney et al. 2017), and are unlikely to engage in thorough assessments of the entrepreneur's background and qualifications (Ciuchta et al. 2016). In 2011, Petty and Gruber delve into the intricacies of the venture capital decision-making process. While previous research has mostly focused on the acceptance criteria employed by venture capitalists, the authors shed light on the often-overlooked aspect of deal rejection criteria. By investigating the dynamics inherent in the venture capital decision-making process, they offer novel insights into this field. This paper presents a qualitative analysis conducted on a rich longitudinal dataset including 11 years of archival data obtained from venture capital companies operating in Europe. During this period, the venture capital firm successfully administered two funds, evaluated a total of 3,631 investment opportunities, and executed 35 investment transactions.

Crowdfunding has many characteristics that have the ability to address the gender disparity seen in traditional fundraising marketplaces. In this context, it is noteworthy to emphasise the deficiency of dependable and authoritative information among crowdfunders. As exemplified by Belleflamme et al. (2014), crowdfunding entails the fundamental concept of entrepreneurs seeking external funds from a vast audience, as opposed to relying on a limited number of seasoned investors. In this model, each individual within the audience, referred to as the "crowd", contributes a nominal sum of money to facilitate the provision of funding. Entrepreneurs leverage existing platforms on social networks and the Internet to engage in direct interactions with large groups of individuals. There exist two distinct variants of crowdfunding: one is consumers placing pre-orders for things, while the other involves individuals making upfront payments in return for a proportionate stake in future revenues. In both scenarios, individuals participating in crowdfunding are provided with community rewards that enhance their utility. The Belleflamme et al. (2014) demonstrate, via the use of a unified model, that entrepreneurs exhibit a preference for engaging in pre-ordering activities when the initial capital requirements are relatively modest, while opting for profit sharing arrangements in cases when the capital requirements are higher. The researchers' findings indicate that it is essential for entrepreneurs to establish a network of persons with whom they can engage, since this has a significant impact on the decision-making processes of management in the initial phases of firm growth. Moss et al. (2015) assert that crowdfunding has emerged as a novel phenomenon that has attracted significant attention from both researchers and practitioners. This heightened interest can be attributed to its perceived value as an alternate means of securing funds. The exponential growth of crowdfunding is accompanied by a corresponding increase in both the obstacles and possibilities associated with this phenomenon. The paper provides a comprehensive analysis of the characteristics of crowdfunding, including associated terminology, essential components, and ethical considerations. Additionally, this study suggests a classification system for crowdfunding and highlights certain challenges that are commonly linked with this practice.

Courtney et al. (2017) emphasise another facet of crowdfunding, which is the absence of human interaction between crowdfunders and project creators. The authors' primary emphasis lies in examining the intricate interplay of signals and confirmations originating from various sources, which have the potential to amplify or diminish other impacts. The use of signals related to start-up behaviour, such as media use, and the presence of elements like crowdfunding experience serve to alleviate worries regarding information asymmetries pertaining to project quality and founder trustworthiness. Consequently, investing in the project can enhance the likelihood of success. Moreover, the present study commences by positing the premise that the signals generated by start-ups exhibit a nullifying effect, but the endorsements from external sources (i.e. emotions conveyed in the comments of supporters) serve to validate and amalgamate the start-up signals.

Nevertheless, it is improbable for crowdfunders to engage in thorough due diligence of the entrepreneur, as demonstrated by Ciuchta et al. (2016). The authors examine this issue using the theory of signals, which posits that attention is often directed towards observable signs. Based on a cognitive framework, this study posits that the manner in which signals are perceived by individuals' intellectual abilities has an impact on the quantity and nature of signals pursued, as well as the duration needed to generate those signals. The research conducted using eye tracking technology demonstrates that individuals participating in equity crowdfunding tend to overlook certain noticeable signals present on campaign pages. Furthermore, variations in the human capital of these crowdfunders have a distinct impact on their ability to create sets of signals.

3.3 The Theory and the Empirical Evidence on the Role of Women in the Equity Crowdfunding

There is emerging evidence indicating a potential advantage for females in certain domains, and many ideas have been proposed to account for this phenomenon.

Certain scholars argue that there is evidence of activist homophily, as demonstrated by Greenberg and Mollick (2017), wherein female supporters exhibit a pronounced preference for projects headed by females as opposed to those led by males. Given the greater representation of women as project creators and funders in comparison with regular markets, it can be inferred that women have a significantly higher likelihood of attaining their financial objectives in informal markets. Nevertheless, it has been seen in several studies (Marom et al. 2016) that males continue to dominate as the primary funders on the majority of crowdfunding platforms. This finding challenges the notion that the female advantage in crowdfunding can be entirely attributed to a demographic impact, hence prompting the exploration of other reasons.

The warm glow theory, as proposed by Andreoni (1990), posits that individuals often engage in acts of assistance or support in order to experience a positive emotional state (Allison et al. 2015). Considering the altruistic tendencies exhibited by crowd investors, it is plausible to posit that they may serve as benefactors for charitable gifts. It is conceivable that these investors may see their investments as having a greater positive impact when directed towards female entrepreneurs, so eliciting a heightened sense of satisfaction in supporting projects headed by women as opposed to those led by males. The differential treatment observed between men and women can be further elucidated by drawing upon the existing body of social psychological literature on stereotypes. It has been established that in situations where individuals have limited access to information, they are more inclined to rely on underlying stereotypes (Tosi and Einbender 1985). Given the nature of crowdfunding markets, it is evident that they exemplify such circumstances. In this particular context, the scholarly literature places emphasis on the examination of stereotypes, specifically in relation to the attribute of trustworthiness (Eckes 2002). Gender, being a prevalent factor in stereotyping, is often seen as a prominent indicator in this regard (Fiske and Taylor 1991). Research in the field of psychology indicates that women are often perceived as possessing higher levels of trustworthiness compared to males. This perception can be attributed to the societal expectations and norms associated with gender roles, particularly those related to domestic responsibilities such as motherhood, which emphasise prioritising the well-being and interests of others.

Drawing from the aforementioned issues, in the following we go more in depth into the findings of the cited studies, exploring in detail the factors that motivate women to participate in crowdfunding.

As underlined, several studies posit that activist homophily plays a prominent role, since empirical evidence suggests that female advocates have a notable inclination towards supporting endeavours spearheaded by other females rather than those led by males. Based on the observed prevalence of women as project developers and funders in informal markets relative to conventional markets, it may be deduced that women possess a notably elevated probability of achieving their financial goals. In their study, Greenberg and Mollick (2017) focus on investigating the factors that influence individuals from underrepresented demographics to assist each other, particularly in the realm of endorsing female entrepreneurs via donation-based crowdfunding initiatives. The notion of attraction-based activist choice homosexuality has been evolved from the premise of selective homophilia. The interconnectedness between two individuals goes beyond just sharing an understanding of shared societal barriers arising from their joint social identities and the formation of solidarity based on group membership. The authors distinguish between activist choice homophilia and homosexuality by analysing the similarities between individuals' "selective homophilia" and "induced homophilia". The operationalisation of the probability of persons belonging to a particular social category engaging in the process of joining and building a network is being discussed. The authors support their activist choice by utilising laboratory experiments and empirical evidence collected from the field. Homophily offers a plausible rationale for the elevated probability of women's success and their superior performance in the crowdfunding industry relative to males, who demonstrate the lowest rates of success in this field. However, it is important to acknowledge that several studies have provided data suggesting that males maintain a dominant position as the primary contributors on the bulk of crowdfunding sites. This implies that the observed benefit of women in crowdfunding cannot be solely attributable to demographic factors, thereby requiring examination of additional explanations. Marom et al. (2016) conducted a study that investigates the time period leading up to and following the formation of a well-known crowdfunding site that operates on a reward-based model, specifically referring to Kickstarter. The activities of entrepreneurs involved in securing pre-seed finance are meticulously documented by the researchers. The phenomenon of women being disproportionately represented in traditionally gendered sectors, such as business and banking, has been observed. The researchers also found that, even after accounting for sectors and funding targets, women had higher rates of achievement in comparison with their male counterparts. Furthermore, it was shown that both male and female supporters exhibited a tendency to favour entrepreneurs who had the same gender as themselves. The use of data from Kickstarter in the current research yields evidence that indicates the existence of preference-based discrimination exhibited by male funders.

The warm glow idea, as proposed by Andreoni (1990), posits that individuals often engage in acts of assistance or support towards others to experience a positive emotional state, specifically when individuals contribute funds towards privately-provided public benefits. In the context of charitable organisations, decision-making processes are influenced by a multitude of considerations beyond the mere consideration of charity. Various psychological factors play a significant role in influencing human behaviour, including social pressure, guilt, compassion, and the intrinsic motivation to experience a positive emotional state sometimes referred to as the "warm glow" effect. The examination of the author delves into the concept of impure altruism in a rigorous manner and explores its wide-ranging ramifications. To fulfil its objective, this article engages in a comprehensive analysis of the immutability thesis pertaining to public goods. It proceeds by establishing the necessary conditions for neutrality to be present, then delving into an examination of the most optimum tax treatment for charitable donations. Furthermore, the research employs econometric techniques to elucidate the underlying mechanisms of policy experiments. The author's analysis reveals that impure altruism aligns more closely with the observed donation patterns compared to classic pure altruism techniques. This finding carries major political implications that diverge from conventional models. It has been determined. According to the research conducted by Allison et al. (2015), micro-loans acquired through crowdfunding serve as a significant means of financial support for individuals with entrepreneurial aspirations. The authors of this study examine the ways in which linguistic cues, which are known to have an impact on underlying motives, might shape an entrepreneur's narrative as either a financial opportunity or a chance to contribute to the welfare of others, drawing on cognitive appraisal theory. Moreover, the researchers conduct an analysis to assess the impact of this framing on the results of fundraising efforts within the domain of pro-social lending. Specifically, they investigate the quantity of micro-loans disbursed via an online crowdfunding platform to a substantial sample of 36,000 entrepreneurs across 51 different nations. The researchers see a favourable response from lenders when narratives emphasise the company's potential to assist others, as opposed to narratives that just focus on commercial prospects.

Based on the aforementioned findings, it can be inferred that crowd investors, due to their altruistic tendencies, have the potential to function as patrons of charitable donations. It is plausible that these investors perceive their investments as having a greater positive impact on female entrepreneurs, leading them to experience a heightened sense of satisfaction when funding projects led by women as opposed to those led by men.

The differential treatment observed between men and women can be further elucidated by referring to the existing body of social psychological literature on stereotypes. In situations where access to comprehensive information is limited, individuals tend to rely on ingrained stereotypes. It is evident that crowdfunding markets exemplify such circumstances. For instance, Tosi and Einbender (1985) conducted a study to examine the idea that judges who have access to a greater amount of job-related information about applicants are more likely to make unbiased choices compared to judges who have access to a lesser amount of job-related information. Since the year 1970, scholarly investigations documented in either the Psychological Abstracts or the Social Science Citation Index have been primarily concerned with examining the quantity of information possessed by judges, as well as the extent to which each piece of knowledge is distinctive to gender. The notion is supported by the findings of the meta-analysis undertaken by the authors. In the present context, the literature pertaining to stereotypes centres its attention on the perception of trustworthiness. For instance, Eckes (2002) conducts an analysis of the paternalistic and jealous gender stereotypes in two separate investigations. Paternalistic stereotypes depict specific subgroups of females and males as possessing warmth without competence, whereas jealous stereotypes depict other subgroups of females and males as having competence without warmth. The study involved the participation of 134 female individuals and 82 male individuals, predominantly belonging to the white ethnic group and middle-class socio-economic background. According to the stereotypic content model proposed by Fiske et al. (2002), the findings of Study 1 indicated that several gender groupings were perceived as possessing high levels of either ability or warmth, while being perceived as having low levels of the other trait. The researchers conducted an experiment to examine the validity of the stereotype hypothesis. Study 2 provided more investigation into the social structure theory, which posits that perceived ability is predicted by status, whereas perceived warmth is predicted by interdependence. The findings of the author provided robust support for both theories. For instance, Fiske and Taylor (1991) propose a perspective that integrates advancements in cognitive psychology pertaining to attention, memory, and reasoning with insights derived from the examination of attitudes, emotions, and motivation. They argue that "social cognition" encompasses the systematic examination and evaluative analysis of theories, empirical evidence, and practical implications centred on the fundamental inquiry of how individuals perceive their social surroundings, with the aim of advancing knowledge in this domain. Research in the field of psychology indicates that women are often perceived as possessing higher levels of trustworthiness compared to males. This perception may be attributed to the societal expectations and conventional social roles that are commonly associated with women, such as their involvement in household responsibilities, exemplified by the position of a mother. These roles are typically characterised by a focus on prioritising the well-being and interests of others.

References

Allison, T. H., Davis, B. C., Short, J. C., and Webb, J. W. (2015). Crowdfunding in a prosocial microlending environment: Examining the role of intrinsic versus extrinsic cues. *Entrepreneurship Theory and Practice*, *39*(1), 53–73.

Andreoni, J. (1990). Impure altruism and donations to public goods: A theory of warm-glow giving. *The Economic Journal*, *100*(401), 464–477.

Belleflamme, P., Lambert, T., and Schwienbacher, A. (2013). Individual crowdfunding practices. *Venture Capital*, *15*(4), 313–333.

Belleflamme, P., Lambert, T., and Schwienbacher, A. (2014). Crowdfunding: Tapping the right crowd. *Journal of Business Venturing*, *29*(5), 585–609.

Belt, B. D., Brummer, C., and Gorfine, D. (2012). *Crowdfunding: Maximizing the promise and minimizing the peril*. Washington, DC: Milken Institute.

Ciuchta, M. P., Letwin, C., Stevenson, R. M., and McMahon, S. R. (2016). Regulatory focus and information cues in a crowdfunding context. *Applied Psychology*, *65*(3), 490–514.

Courtney, C., Dutta, S., and Li, Y. (2017). Resolving information asymmetry: Signaling, endorsement, and crowdfunding success. *Entrepreneurship Theory and Practice*, *41*(2), 265–290.

De Buysere, K., Gajda, O., Kleverlaan, R., Marom, D., and Klaes, M. (2012). A framework for European crowdfunding.

Eckes, T. (2002). Paternalistic and envious gender stereotypes: Testing predictions from the stereotype content model. *Sex Roles*, *47*(3/4), 99.

Fiske, S. T., and Taylor, S. E. (1991). *Social cognition*. McGraw-Hill Book Company.

Fiske, S. T., Cuddy, A. J., Glick, P., and Xu, J. (2002). A model of (often mixed) stereotype content: Competence and warmth respectively follow from perceived status and competition. *Journal of Personality and Social Psychology*, *82*(6), 878.

Greenberg, J., and Mollick, E. (2017). Activist choice homophily and the crowdfunding of female founders. *Administrative Science Quarterly*, *62*(2), 341–374.

Harrington, K. (2014, February 7). *Cashing in on crowdfunding*. Forbes, Entrepreneurs.

Hemer, J. (2011). *A snapshot on crowdfunding* (No. R2/2011). Arbeitspapiere Unternehmen und Region.

Ingram, C., and Teigland, R. (2013). *Crowdfunding among IT Entrepreneurs in Sweden*. Stockholm: Stockholm School of Economics.

Lebraty, J. F., and Lobre-Lebraty, K. (2013). *Crowdsourcing: One step beyond*. Wiley.

Marom, D., Robb, A., and Sade, O. (2016). *Gender Dynamics in Crowdfunding (Kickstarter): Evidence on entrepreneurs, investors, deals and taste-based discrimination*. Investors, Deals and Taste-Based Discrimination.

Massolution, C. L. (2012). Crowdfunding industry report: Market trends, composition and crowdfunding platforms.

Mollick, E. (2014). The dynamics of crowdfunding: An exploratory study. *Journal of Business Venturing, 29*(1), 1–16.

Moss, T. W., Neubaum, D. O., and Meyskens, M. (2015). The effect of virtuous and entrepreneurial orientations on microfinance lending and repayment: A signaling theory perspective. *Entrepreneurship Theory and Practice, 39*(1), 27–52.

Petty, J. S., and Gruber, M. (2011). "In pursuit of the real deal": A longitudinal study of VC decision making. *Journal of Business Venturing*, *26*(2), 172–188.

Rubinton, B. J. (2011). Crowdfunding: Disintermediated investment banking. Available at SSRN 1807204.

Steinberg, M. (2012). *Anime's media mix: Franchising toys and characters in Japan*. University of Minnesota Press.

Tosi, H. L., and Einbender, S. W. (1985). The effects of the type and amount of information in sex discrimination research: A meta-analysis. *Academy of Management Journal*, *28*(3), 712–723.

Wicks, M. (2013). *Crowdfunding-an introduction*. Victoria: Blue Beetle Books.

CHAPTER 4

An Empirical Investigation on the Italian Context

Francesca Battaglia

Abstract This chapter presents an empirical cross-platform analysis of the Italian equity crowdfunding context over the period 2014–2020, aiming to explore the relationship between female entrepreneurs and the success of the campaigns. In more detail, we aim to investigate if female-led equity crowdfunding campaigns are more successful than male ones.

Keywords Empirical cross-platform analysis · Italian equity crowdfunding platforms · Italian regulation · Female entrepreneurs · Success of female-led campaigns · Univariate analysis · Tobit regression · Negative binomial regression · Robustness check

Equity crowdfunding is emerging as an innovative form of raising capital and it is an alternative to the traditional lending channel for start-ups and early-stage companies. We decide to focus on Italy for several reasons. First of all, Italy is the first country in the world to have a specific discipline on equity crowdfunding in order to increase the number of firms relying on this alternative funding channel and of the potential investors (Ahlers et al. 2015). These regulatory reforms play a central role in the Italian financial system, as it is mainly based on small and medium-sized

F. Battaglia and E. Giusi Gaeta, *Women in Alternative Finance*,
https://doi.org/10.1007/978-3-031-43467-9_4

enterprises. This issue will be examined in the next sub-section. Moreover, although the growth of the Italian crowdfunding markets is marginal compared to countries like the United States or the United Kingdom, in recent years it has experienced a very strong growth: Crowdfunding Buzz shows that in 2018 the Italian equity crowdfunding platforms collected more than three times the amount gathered in 2017, with more than twice the number of successful campaigns. The overall volumes were well above expectations: total fundraising exceeded 36 million euros in 2018 (11.7 million in 2017) and 114 companies were financed (50 in 2017). The number of investors also tripled, from around 3,300 in 2017 to almost 9,500 in 2018. In the first quarter of 2019, equity crowdfunding in Italy beat all records: 135 million fundraising, 35 funded companies, 5 campaigns over 1 million, and 2 above the 2 million. Furthermore, also the COVID-19 pandemic has highlighted the crucial role of women in leadership positions (i.e. Gorbatai and Nelson 2015; Horvat and Papamarkou 2017; Malaga et al. 2018; McGuire 2020; Bapna and Ganco 2018; Barbi and Mattioli 2019).

Psychology shows that women tend to be viewed as more trustworthy than men because of typical social roles that society associates with women, like domestic roles (e.g. mother, secretary) whose purpose is to put the goodwill of others first. Because of the high levels of uncertainty in crowdfunding, trustworthiness perceptions should play a central role in the crowdfunding context. Moreover, referring to this concern, we think that perceived trustworthiness could be higher in those countries where women still play traditional role and where social customs put women in the home, doing housework and caring for children and elderly, while men are responsible to work and bring home money to support the family.

4.1 The Italian Equity Crowdfunding Context

According to the Crowd-Investing Observatory at MIP, the School of Management of Politecnico di Milano (osservatoriocrowdinvesting.it), the overall capital raised by Italian companies through crowdfunding platforms is €908 million as of June 2020. In particular, as reported in Fig. 4.1, €158.9 million is the capital raised through equity-based platforms.

According to the "5° Report italiano sul CrowdInvesting" (2020), there are 42 authorised equity-based crowdfunding platforms in Italy.

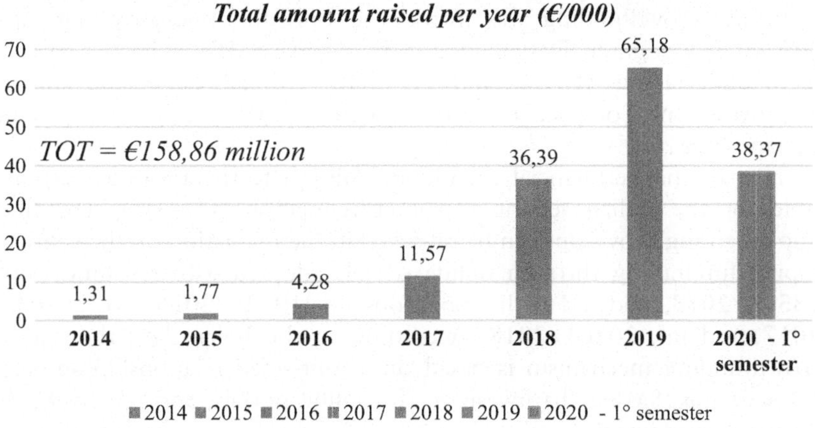

Fig. 4.1 Trend of successful equity crowdfunding campaigns in Italy from 2014 to 2020 (*Source* Crowd-Investing Observatory report, July 2020)

The equity raised in the period June 2019–June 2020 is €76.6 million, +56% compared to the previous year (€49 million). The trend is still positive despite COVID-19: the observatory reports a 40% growth in the first semester 2020, compared to Q1 2019. On average, the equity raised per campaign is €192,481, with a 72.7% success rate (75% in the first semester 2020). These numbers do not consider the real estate equity crowdfunding platforms, which on average raise €804,914 per campaign. Companies raising capital are primary innovative start-ups (58%), innovative SMEs (13%), and then "traditional" SMEs and investment vehicles. Capital is needed mainly for marketing investments (49%) and product development (30%). If we look at the investment size, the average ticket is €3,222 for individuals and €20,000 for corporates. As of 30 June 2020, the value of the overall portfolio increased by 10.41% compared the estimated value in the previous year.

4.2 The Italian Regulation

Between 2012 and 2013 (Law 221/2012), Italy was the first country in the world to regulate the equity crowdfunding market, also through the creation of a special register of authorised online portals.

Equity crowdfunding was introduced only for innovative start-ups initially. It was gradually extended to innovative SMEs, collective investment undertakings (CIUs), and VC funds (Law 33/2015, also known as "Investment Compact") and then, with the 2017 Budget Law, to all Italian SMEs.

This alternative financial channel has subject to the authority responsible for the Italian securities market regulation (Consob). The first implementing provisions can be retrieved in the regulation on the venture capital fundraising through online portals adopted with resolution no. 18592/2013, updated with resolutions no. 19520/2016, no. 20204/2017, and no. 20264/2018. According to the Italian law, the equity crowdfunding mechanism is based on a four-sided relationship among: (a) start-ups/SMEs, (b) investors, (c) online portals, and (d) banks or investment companies.

Equity crowdfunding is so available for: (a) innovative start-ups that meet requisites outlined in Law 221/2012 and that are enrolled in a special section of the Companies Register, (b) innovative SMEs that meet requisites outlined in Law 33/2015, and (c) since 2017, it was extended to all Italian SMEs (ex EU recommendation no. 2003/361). Such companies are allowed to offer their capital to the public through online crowdfunding platforms, registered in a special register held by CONSOB (Register of Platforms), provided that the overall amount of shares or quotas offered does not exceed EUR 5 million. There is no maximum number of shareholders or investors, and to close the funding operation, at least 5% of the equity securities must be subscribed by professional investors, banks, or incubators of the start-up. In this regard, the main purpose of the equity crowdfunding regulation is not only to help newly incorporated companies to raise funds in an easy and informal way by allowing non- professional investors access to public offers, but it seems also to aim at protecting such investors by simplifying and facilitating the entire process of investment.

In particular, innovative start-ups are companies which: *(i)* are not listed on a regulated market; *(ii)* have started their activity by no more than 60 months; *(iii)* have their registered office in Italy or a branch or a production facility in Italy; *(iv)* have total turnover of maximum EUR 5,000,000; *(v)* have as exclusive company object the manufacturing and marketing of innovative products or services which are highly innovative.

Moreover, an innovative start-up is a company that meets at least one of the three following requirements: *(i)* expenses relating to R&D

equal or above the 15% of the higher between turnover and cost of the production; *(ii)* part of the employees shall have to be graduated with a three-year research experience or with a university research experience; *(iii)* ownership of IP rights referring to industrial patent, biotech, new plant-related kind, or original software code.

Innovative SMEs are companies which: *(i)* are not listed on a regulated market, but which can have the shares traded on MTF; *(ii)* have their registered office in Italy or a branch or a production facility in Italy; *(iii)* have independent firm revision of the last available balance sheet. In addition, an innovative SME must comply with at least two of the following three requirements: *(i)* expenses relating to R&D equal or above the 3% of the higher between turnover and cost of the production; *(ii)* part of the employees shall have to be graduated with a three-year research experience or with a university research experience; *(iii)* ownership of IP rights referring to industrial patent, biotech, new plant-related kind or original software code.

Only companies duly registered with a new register kept by Consob can operate as online portals. In order to be enrolled in this register, companies shall submit specific documents to Consob, allowing the latter to verify that they meet the requirements provided by the new regulation. Companies admitted to operate as online portals will be subject to ongoing monitoring activity by Consob and they will not be entitled to perform any investment services, nor to take care of any payment made by the investors to finalise their subscription.

The main goal of the last regulatory updates (resolutions no. 19520/2016, no. 20204/2017, and no. 20264/2018) is not only to reduce the companies' costs of collecting money through online funding portals, but also to increase the number of firms relying on this alternative funding channel and of the potential investors, by including business angels in the definition of professional investors in order to meet the 5% threshold of the shares held by them. These regulatory reforms play a central role in the Italian financial system, as it is mainly based on small and medium-sized enterprises. Between 2014 and 2018, overall SMEs' value added increased, rising by 12.4%. It exceeded its 2008 pre-crisis level by 3.3%. In 2018, SMEs generated 66.9% of overall value added in the Italian "non-financial business economy", exceeding the EU average of 56.4%.

Moreover, while credit has become more easily available for some SMEs, other segments of the SME population still face substantial difficulties in accessing debt finance. Transaction costs are particularly high in relative terms for micro-enterprises, start-ups, young SMEs, innovative firms, and businesses located in remote and/or rural areas, potentially excluding them from any sources of formal external financing. Evidence suggests that financial institutions have become more risk-averse compared to the pre-crisis period, and that the financing constraints of these firms may have become more structurally entrenched. Against this backdrop, the long-standing need to strengthen SME capital structures and decrease their dependence on the banking borrowing channel has become more urgent. It is therefore crucial to improve SMEs' access to alternative sources of finance, like equity crowdfunding.

4.3 The Empirical Analysis

In this section, we present our empirical analysis of the Italian equity crowdfunding context over the period 2014–2020, aiming to explore the relationship between female entrepreneurs and the success of the campaigns. In more detail, we aim to investigate if female-led equity crowdfunding campaigns are more successful than male ones.

4.3.1 Sample and Data Sources

We conduct a cross-platform analysis by investigating equity crowdfunding local platforms operating in Italy from January 2014 to June 2020. Our sample is all-encompassing of all the cases on the Italian platforms (successful and unsuccessful campaigns). We build up a hand-collected dataset of 437 equity crowdfunding campaigns pitched on equity crowdfunding platforms active in Italy, at the date of data collection (the end of June 2020). The list of Italian authorised equity crowdfunding platforms is from the CONSOB registry. All the authorised equity crowdfunding platforms, according to the Italian regulation, are registered on this list. Our sample refers to the following 21 platforms with active campaigns: Action Crowd, Back To Work 24, Cofyp, Crowd-FundMe, CrowdInvest, Ecomill, Extrafin, Forcrowd, Fundera, Idea Crowdfunding, Investi-re, Leonardo equity, Lita.co, Mamacrowd, Muum Lab, Next Equity, OpStart, Stars Up, The Best Equity, 200Crowd, and We Are Starting.

The online portal provides investors with specific and detailed information about the start-up and the public offer. Such measures are designed to ensure that potential investors are fully aware of the risks of their investments. The information reported in the public offer available on the online portal is not subject to the Consob approval, as each start-up is responsible for its reliability, truthfulness, and accuracy. The analysed platforms work according to the traditional "All-or-Nothing" model (Cumming et al. 2015); thus, a project is considered successful or funded only if the 100% of the funding goal or more is reached within the planned time period. If at the end of the campaign the funding goal is reached, the invested amounts are transferred from the escrow accounts to the founders' accounts and, consequently, investors become shareholders of the company; if not, the platforms refund the invested amount to investors. The platforms' websites display all the successful campaigns in a clear and consistent format across all pitches.

The list of the investigated platforms is reported in Table 4.1, which shows the city in which the platform is located, its foundation year, and the registration date.

Table 4.1 Italian equity crowdfunding platforms

Platform	*City*	*Foundation year*	*Registration date*
Action Crowd	Milan	2012	26/02/2014
BackToWork (ex Equinvest)	Milan	2014	14/01/2015
Cofyp	Macerata	2016	14/04/2016
CrowdFundMe	Milan	2013	30/07/2014
CrowdInvest Italia	Prato	2018	10/07/2018
Ecomill	Milan	2014	29/10/2014
Extrafin	Udine	2018	05/07/2018
Forcrowd	Milano	2019	12/06/2019
Fundera	Milan	2014	10/09/2014
Idea Crowdfunding	Rome	2017	29/11/2017
Investi-RE	Milan	2015	28/01/2015
Leonardo Equity	Florence	2018	17/04/2018
LITA.co Italy (ex 1001PACT.com)	Torino	2018	31/05/2018
Mamacrowd	Milan	2014	06/08/2014
Muum Lab	Lecce	2015	06/08/2014
Next Equity	Macerata	2014	16/07/2014
OpStart	Bergamo	2015	11/11/2015
Stars Up	Livorno	2013	18/10/2013
The Best Equity	Milan	2018	14/03/2018
Two-Hundred – 200 Crowd	Brescia	2014	18/06/2014
We Are Starting	Bergamo	2014	16/12/2014

We gather information on equity crowdfunding campaigns both from the website of each platform and from the original offering documents of the project, where they are recorded and publicly available.

To ensure that investors are fully aware of the risks associated with their investment, the online portal has to provide them with specific and detailed information on the start-up and public offer. Once the campaign is ended, invested amounts are transferred from the escrow accounts to the founders' accounts. After that, investors become shareholders in the company, and they acquire all the established rights. Conversely, when the funding goal is not reached, the platforms will refund the invested amount to investors. All the successful campaigns are displayed on platforms' websites following a similar structure, ensuring homogeneity and comparability for the collected information.

We collected information on the features of the offers and on the founders' profiles, as reported on the "Team" page of each campaign. The public data available has some limitations. Some information referring to the identity of the investors, founders, and CEOs' start-up is incomplete or unavailable. Moreover, many platforms allow investors to invest in a crowdfunding campaign by using the "Anonymous" identity.

4.3.2 Variables

Since our aim is to investigate the role of female entrepreneurs on the success of equity crowdfunding projects, our dependent variable is a proxy for the campaign success. Following prior studies on the topic (e.g. Vismara 2016; Colombo et al. 2015; Ahlers et al. 2015), we measure success in three different ways: (1) the (natural log of) number of investors (*number of investors*), (2) the (natural log) of the amount raised at the end of each campaign (*amount raised*), and (3) a dichotomous measure of campaign's success (*success*) equal to 1 for campaigns reaching or exceeding their capital, and 0 otherwise. To test our hypotheses, we include a comprehensive list of explanatory variables, which are in line with the crowdfunding literature (see Table 4.2).

Our main interest variable is related to female entrepreneurship as a driver of campaign success (i.e. Mohammadi and Shafi, 2017; Horvat and Papamarkou 2017; Malaga et al. 2018; McGuire 2020; Bapna and Ganco 2018; Barbi and Mattioli 2019): *female founders* is a dummy variable, taking the value of 1 if at least one founder is woman, and 0 otherwise.

Table 4.2 Variable definitions

Variable name	*Description*
Dependent variables	
Success	Dummy variable equal to 1 for campaigns reaching or exceeding their capital, and 0 otherwise
Amount raised (€)	The total amount raised at the end of the campaign
Number of investors	The number of investors at the end of the campaign
Explanatory variables	
Female founders	Dummy variable equal to 1 if the founder is a woman, and 0 otherwise
Control variables	
Equity offered (%)	Percentage of equity offered by founders to external investors
Social capital	Number of proponent's LinkedIn connections
Covid	Dummy variable equal to 1 if the project has been launched during the outbreak, and 0 otherwise
Financial info	Dummy variable equal to 1 if financial information on the company are available on the platform, and 0 otherwise
Patent	Dummy variable indicating whether a start-up quotes a granted patent in an offering document. The variable equals 1 if so, and 0 otherwise
Number of comments	Number of comments on the project page
Team's education level	Dummy which takes the value of 1 if there is at least one team member with an high academic status (i.e. university degree, PhD or the title of Professor) within the company, and 0 otherwise
Target capital (€)	Amount of target capital to be raised

Note This table shows the variables used in our empirical analysis, distinguishing by dependent, explanatory, and control variables

We include in our regression models a set of additional control variables to account for other factors that, following previous studies, might be a relevant driver of success for equity-based crowdfunding campaigns.

Since our investigated time horizon spans from 2014 to 2020, by including the COVID-19 pandemic, we insert in our analysis the interaction term *female founders_covid* between the dummy *covid* and the value of *female founders*. We do not include the value of the *covid* variable standing alone, since its effect would be not distinguishable from other factors that are country-specific and time-variant.

The relative percentage of equity offered to investors (*equity offered*) in each offering is measured as in Ahlers et al. (2015) and Vismara (2016). The amount of equity offered is reported on the main web page of each campaign. The recent literature on success factors for crowdfunding (Block et al. 2018; Guenther et al. 2018; Angerer et al. 2017; Piva and Rossi-Lamastra 2018; Vismara 2016, 2018a; Hornuf and Neuenkirch 2016; Lukkarinen et al. 2016; Ralcheva and Roosenboom 2019; Vulkan et al. 2016; Agrawal et al. 2015; Ahlers et al. 2015) finds that the share of equity retained by founders is a quality signal of the campaign, able to reduce the information asymmetries faced by crowdfunding investors and to help founders to achieve the fundraising goal. Moreover, also social capital (*social capital*) plays a relevant role in the setting of the equity crowdfunding campaign. In detail, many papers (Piva and Rossi-Lamastra 2018; Vismara 2016; Ahlers et al. 2015; Mollick 2014; Lin et al. 2012; Ordanini et al. 2011; Sørensen and Fassiotto 2011; Stam and Elfring 2008; Shane and Cable 2002) highlight that a larger number of entrepreneurs' social network connections increase the probability of fundraising success. Mollick (2014), Colombo et al. (2015), and Piva and Rossi-Lamastra (2018) use social networks as proxies of social capital; accordingly, we record the number of connections of each founder on his LinkedIn profile, and then, we calculate the number of the LinkedIn connections of all founders to build our variable *Social capital*.

In line with Ralcheva and Roosenboom (2019), Vismara (2018b), and Piva and Rossi-Lamastra (2018), we include as a measure of intellectual capital, *patent*, which is captured by a dummy variable equal to 1 if a venture possesses, or has applied for a patent, and 0 otherwise. To measure the effectiveness of the intellectual capital, we look at whether the offering document of the analysed start-up reports a granted patent. Moreover, we include *team's education level* (Barbi and Mattioli 2019; Piva and Rossi-Lamastra 2018), a dummy variable which takes the value of 1 if there is at least one team member with a high academic status (such as university degree, PhD or the title of "Professor") within the company, and 0 otherwise.

Then, we consider other control variables to take into account the riskiness of the proposal perceived by investors. Entrepreneurs have the opportunity to include in the offering document a more precise and detailed overview of the risks of the project, in order to provide investors a wider information set to formulate their expectations (e.g. Epstein and Schneider 2008). According to the empirical evidence, investors consider the disclosure of a disclaimer as a quality signal of the campaign. For this reason, we include in our regression models the variable *financial info*, which is equal to 1 if financial information on the company are available on the platform and 0 otherwise.

We consider also the "size" of the campaign, proxied by its fundraising goal (*target capital*), measured as the amount (millions of euros) that founders seek to raise through the crowdfunding campaign (Block et al. 2018; Mollick 2014). Finally, as all the campaigns posted on the platform include the possibility to comment the project, we consider number of comments (*Number of comments*) on the project page. Many authors (Kunz et al. 2016; Vismara 2018b; Angerer et al. 2017; Block et al. 2018) find that the presence of a product video, the images quality, and the comments or updates increase the campaigns success probability.

4.3.3 *Univariate Analysis*

Table 4.3 reports the descriptive statistics of the variables used in our regression analysis. Our sample consists of 437 campaigns conducted through the overall Italian platforms between January 2014 and June 2020. The average project in our sample raises about 135% (€241,384) of the target capital from 80 investors (Table 4.3). Some projects attracted more than 2000 investors and raised more than three times their targets. About 77% of the Italian crowdfunding campaigns have been successful, while 23% of them have failed.

Our key independent variable is *female founders*, a dummy variable equal to 1 if the founder is a woman, and 0 otherwise. In our sample, about 42% of funders (almost half) are women, while about half of the team members (49%) have a high academic status (i.e. university degree, a PhD, the title of Professor). The average equity offered at listing is 8.43% and the average target capital is €178,788. The average entrepreneur in our sample has 424 LinkedIn connections, by highlighting that the social connections are crucial in our sample. The number of the project's comments ranges from 0 to 123, with an average of 13.8. In our sample, less than half (35%) of firms have a patent, and about 59% of them provide a full disclosure of their financial information.

4.3.4 *Estimation Model and Results*

Following Piva and Rossi-Lamastra (2018), we first run a Tobit regression for the amount of capital raised from a project (Model 1), and then, following Ahlers et al. (2015) and Vismara (2016), we run a negative

Table 4.3 Descriptive statistics

	# Observation	*Mean*	*Std. Dev.*	*Min*	*Max*
Dependent variables					
Success	437	0.771167	0.4205629	0	1
Amount raised	437	241,384.5	254,255.3	0	3,435,500
Number of investors	437	79.7	84.3231	0	2,080
Explanatory variables					
Female founders	437	0.4184646	0.4502289	0	1
Control variables					
Equity offered	437	8.431851	7.066955	0.02	40
Social capital	437	424.9011	323.328	1	3,389
Covid	79	1	0	0	1
Financial info	437	0.5860465	0.4931141	0	1
Patent	437	0.3496333	0.4774381	0	1
Number of comments	437	13.86702	18.00143	0	123
Team's education level	437	0.486513	0.382134	0	1
Target capital (€)	437	178,788.2	15,3216.8	18,000	2,200,000

Note This table shows the descriptive statistics of our sample of crowdfunding campaigns launched on the Italian platforms from January 2014 to June 2020. Amount raised and Target capital are expressed in Euros. Success, Female Founders, Financial info, Patent, and Team's education level are binary variables that take the value 1 if there is the presence of the qualitative attribute. Number of investors is expressed in absolute terms. Social capital is calculated as the number of the LinkedIn connections of all founders. Number of comments reports the number of comments on the project page expressed in absolute terms. Equity offered is the percentage of equity offered

binomial regression (Model 2), since the number of investors is measured as a count variable. As robustness check, we run a logistic regression by using a dichotomous measure of campaign's success (Model 3), equal to 1 for campaigns reaching or exceeding their capital (Ahlers et al. 2015; Colombo et al. 2015; Vismara 2016) and 0 otherwise. Since this variable present some very large outliers, we winsorise values at the 99th percentile (for a similar approach, see Ahlers et al. 2015; Vismara 2016; Vulkan et al. 2016; Piva and Rossi-Lamastra 2018).

Our models incorporate both year fixed effects, capturing unobservable factors which are time-variant and may have an effect on crowdfunding campaigns (i.e. the degree of crowdfunding legitimacy over time, economic cycle…), and platform fixed effects, in order to account for unobserved time invariant heterogeneity across several platforms. Robust standard errors are clustered at industry level.

Table 4.4 shows the results of the first econometric analysis, with dependent variables measuring crowdfunding campaign's success. In Model 1, the campaign success is measured by using the amount raised; in Model 2, we use as proxy of campaign's success the (natural log of) total number of investors at the end of the campaign, while in Model 3 our dependent variable is the dummy variable *success*. Our results show that women entrepreneurs perform well in the equity crowdfunding scenario, since the dummy *female founders* has always a strong and positive effect on the amount raised at the end of the campaign with respect to the goal (Model 1, coefficient = 0.432, significant at 1%) on the number of investors (Model 2, coefficient = 0.162, significant at 1%) and on the probability of the campaign's success (Model 3, coefficient = 0.231, significant at 1%). By analysing the interaction term between *female founders* and *covid*, our findings show that there has been an increase in successful role of female entrepreneurs during the COVID-19 pandemic period. Specifically, all the coefficients of this variable are strongly and positively associated with the campaign's success (Model 1, coefficient = 0.460; Model 2, coefficient = 0.234; Model 3, coefficient = 0.365, always significant at 1% confidence level).

In the Italian equity crowdfunding context, *female founders* may be considered more trustworthy than men counterparty because of typical social roles, like domestic roles (e.g. mother) whose purpose is to put the goodwill of others first, that society associates to them. According to Gorbatai and Nelson (2015), women are more prone to use a highly communicative language that makes them capable of reaching a broad consensus among potential investors. Our findings are also in line with Horvat and Papamarkou (2017), Malaga et al. (2018), McGuire (2020), and Bapna and Ganco (2018) who show that female entrepreneurs benefit of higher success rates in fundraising.

Referring to our control variable, our results show that, in line with Ahlers et al. (2015), Vismara (2016), Ralcheva and Roosenboom (2019), in all our model specifications a larger percentage of equity offered is associated with a smaller amount of capital raised (Model 1, coefficient = −0.856, significant at 1%), a lower number of investors (Model 2, coefficient = −0.245, significant at 1%), and a reduced likelihood of campaign's success (Model 3, coefficient = −0.499, significant at 5%). According to this evidence, we can argue that the amount of equity retained by

Table 4.4 Determinants of the amount raised, number of investors, and success

Variables	*(Model 1) Amount raised*	*(Model 2) Number of investors*	*(Model 3) Success*
Female founders	0.432***	0.162***	0.231***
	(0.167)	(0.0208)	(0.134)
Female founders_covid	0.460***	0.234***	0.365***
	(0.134)	(0.0283)	(0.123)
Equity offered	−0.856***	−0.243***	−0.499**
	(0.0211)	(0.0285)	(0.221)
Social capital	0.000245***	0.000338***	0.0301***
	(0.0000223)	(0.0000467)	(0.00393)
Financial info	0.225	0.132	0.636*
	(0.735)	(0.175)	(0.224)
Patent	0.246***	0.247**	1.022**
	(0.132)	(0.0321)	(0.314)
Number of comments	0.0435***	0.0564***	0.134***
	(0.00398)	(0.00732)	(0.0143)
Team's education level	0.244***	0.236**	0.255*
	(0.432)	(0.217)	(0.489)
Target capital	0.254	0.0368	1.267
	(0.141)	(0.0601)	(0.934)
Constant	5.122***	2.421***	15.72**
	(3.223)	(0.548)	(10.34)
lnalpha		−2.016***	
		(0.127)	
Observations	437	437	437
Year fixed effect	Yes	Yes	Yes
Platform fixed effect	Yes	Yes	Yes
Adj. R-squared	0.3516	0.1436	0.5443

Robust standard errors in parentheses; ***$p < 0.01$, **$p < 0.05$, *$p < 0.1$

Note The table reports the coefficients of our empirical analysis with all variables winsorised at the 3rd and the 97th percentiles. Model 1 reports the coefficient of a Tobit regression of Ln (Amount Raised), i.e. the natural logarithm of the amount raised by the company at the end of the campaign, on the chosen explanatory variables. Model 2 reports the coefficients of a negative binomial regression of Number of Investors, on the chosen explanatory variables. Model 3 reports the coefficient of a logit regression in which the dependent variable is Success, a binary variable that identifies the success of equity crowdfunding projects. In each analysis, we include the key independent variables referring to the number of female company's founders (female founders). We also include a set of control variables, such as, the interaction term between female founders and covid (female founders_covid), equity offered (equity offered), social network information (social capital), the financial information (financial info), the granted patents (patent), the number of comments on the project page (number of comments), the team's academic status (team's education level), and the information related to the target amount (target capital). The variables equity offered, social capital, number of comments, and target capital are standardised. All the model specifications include year and platform fixed effects. Standard errors (in brackets) are clustered at industry level (sectors are defined by the NACE codes). ***, **, or * denote significance at the 1%, 5%, and 10% levels, respectively founders is perceived as a quality signal of the crowdfunding campaign by external investors.

Referring to *social capital*, consistently with prior research (i.e. Piva and Rossi-Lamastra 2018; Lukkarinen et al. 2016; Vismara 2016; Ahlers et al. 2015), our findings also show that the founders' LinkedIn connections positively and significantly affect the amount raised, the number of investors, and the campaign's success probability, at the 1% confidence level.

We also find that the number of comments on the project page has a positive impact on the equity crowdfunding campaigns. In detail, in all our model specifications, the number of comments is always significant at 1%. This result is consistent with previous studies focusing on the relationship among the campaigns success probability and additional documents posted on the project page (i.e. videos, presentations, comments) useful for investors (i.e. Kunz et al. 2016; Vismara 2018b; Angerer et al. 2017; Block et al. 2018; Piva and Rossi-Lamastra 2018). Moreover, *patent* has a strongly positive impact both on the investor's decision to fund a project and on the amount raised, and it is also positively related to the likelihood of success (i.e. Barbi and Mattioli 2019; Ralcheva and Roosenboom 2019; Piva and Rossi-Lamastra 2018; Hoenig and Henkel 2015). Finally, consistent with the literature on the topic (i.e. Barbi and Mattioli 2019; Piva and Rossi-Lamastra 2018), the education level of the team members launching the campaign is positive and statistically significant at the 10% confidence level or less in all our empirical models, by playing an important role on the probability of the success of the projects.

4.4 Main Implications of Results

Female entrepreneurs are less likely to receive private equity funding, institutional capital, and bank financing in traditional markets. This makes the weight of female entrepreneurship strictly minority in some fields. The difficult to access to traditional credit sources may lead female entrepreneurs to actively seek funding from alternative channels, such as crowdfunding. There is some early evidence that women are not at a disadvantage compared to men in crowdfunding, and they even seem to perform better (e.g. Zhao et al. 2020; Johnson et al. 2018; Mollick and Robb 2016). In Italy, the investment-based crowdfunding industry has been developing relatively fast over the last few years. This chapter aims to provide new empirical evidence on the relationship between female entrepreneurship and equity crowdfunding in the Italian scenario. By using a dataset of 437 equity crowdfunding campaigns, gathered from the crowdfunding local platforms operating in Italy from January 2014 to June 2020, we find that women have an advantage with respect to men and they perform well in the equity crowdfunding scenario. Specifically, in line with McGuire (2020), Bapna and Ganco (2018), Malaga et al. (2018), and Horvat and Papamarkou (2017), equity crowdfunding female-led campaigns significantly outperform those led by men in terms of probability of success. Moreover, also in this period of great uncertainty triggered by COVID-19, female founders may be considered more trustworthy than men counterparty because of typical social roles, like domestic roles (e.g. mother) whose purpose is to put the goodwill of others first that society associates to them. According to Gorbatai and Nelson (2015), women are more prone to use a highly communicative language that makes them capable of reaching a broad consensus among potential investors. In a similar vein, backers are more likely to be ideally linked to figures (like mothers) caring about others. This result highlights that equity crowdfunding may be an effective funding channel for female entrepreneurship, especially in countries where this is still less developed than male one, giving a significant contribution to the path towards gender equality. Moreover, our findings have practical implications for starts-ups and crowdfunding platforms: for both, it is worthwhile to learn more about the factors perceived by potential investors as a quality signal of the project, in order to increase the likelihood of a successful campaign and, ultimately, the platform' own business success. It also has important policy implications, providing regulators with further evidence in favour of facilitating the development of alternative finance and creating a level playing field across European countries.

References

Agrawal, A., Catalini, C., & Goldfarb, A. (2015). Crowdfunding: Geography, social networks, and the timing of investment decisions. *Journal of Economics & Management Strategy, 24*(2), 253–274.

Ahlers, G. K., Cumming, D., Günther, C., and Schweizer, D. (2015). Signaling in equity crowdfunding. *Entrepreneurship Theory and Practice, 39*(4), 955–980.

Angerer, M., Brem, A., Kraus, S., and Peter, A. (2017). Start-up funding via equity crowdfunding in Germany: A qualitative analysis of success factors. *The Journal of Entrepreneurial Finance, 19*(1), 1–34.

Bapna, S., and Ganco, M. (2018). Gender gaps in equity crowdfunding: Evidence from a randomized field experiment. *Management Science, 7*, 1–32. https://doi.org/10.1287/mnsc.2020.3644.

Barbi, M., and Mattioli, S. (2019). Human capital, investor trust, and equity crowdfunding. *Research in International Business and Finance*, *49*, 1–12.

Block, J., Hornuf, L., and Moritz, A. (2018). Which updates during an equity crowdfunding campaign increase crowd participation? *Small Business Economics, 50*(1), 3–27.

Colombo, M. G., Franzoni, C., and Rossi–Lamastra, C. (2015). Internal social capital and the attraction of early contributions in crowdfunding. *Entrepreneurship Theory and Practice*, *39*(1), 75–100.

Cumming, D. J., Leboeuf, G., and Schwienbacher, A. (2015). *Crowdfunding models: Keep-it-all vs*. Available at SSRN 2447567.

Epstein, L. G., and Schneider, M. (2008). Ambiguity, information quality, and asset pricing. *The Journal of Finance*, *63*(1), 197–228.

Gorbatai, A., and Nelson, L. (2015). *The narrative advantage: Gender and the language of crowdfunding*. Haas School of Business UC Berkeley. Research Papers, 1–32.

Guenther, C., Johan, S., and Schweizer, D. (2018). Is the crowd sensitive to distance?—How investment decisions differ by investor type. *Small Business Economics, 50*, 289–305.

Hoenig, D., and Henkel, J. (2015). Quality signals? The role of patents, alliances, and team experience in venture capital financing. *Research Policy, 44*(5), 1049–1064.

Hornuf, L., and Neuenkirch, M. (2016). Pricing shares in equity crowdfunding. *Research Papers in Economics*, (7/15).

Horvat, E. A., and Papamarkou, T. (2017, September). Gender differences in equity crowdfunding. In *Proceedings of the AAAI conference on human computation and crowdsourcing* (Vol. 5, pp. 51–60).

Johnson, M. A., Stevenson, R. M., and Letwin, C. R. (2018). A woman's place is in the… startup! Crowdfunder judgments, implicit bias, and the stereotype content model. *Journal of Business Venturing*, *33*(6), 813–831.

Kunz, M. M., Englisch, O., Beck, J., & Bretschneider, U. (2016). Sometimes you win, sometimes you learn: Success factors in reward-based crowdfunding. *Multikonferenz Wirtschaftsinformatik (MKWI), Ilmenau, 2016*, 467–478.

Lin, M., Prabhala, N. R., and Viswanathan, S. (2013). Judging borrowers by the company they keep: Friendship networks and information asymmetry in online peer-to-peer lending. *Management science, 59*(1), 17–35.

Lukkarinen, A., Teich, J. E., Wallenius, H., and Wallenius, J. (2016). Success drivers of online equity crowdfunding campaigns. *Decision Support Systems*, *87*, 26–38.

Malaga, R., Mamonov, S., and Rosenblum, J. (2018). Gender difference in equity crowdfunding: An exploratory analysis. *International Journal of Gender and Entrepreneurship, 10*(4), 332–343.

McGuire, E. (2020). Can equity crowdfunding close the gender gap in startup finance? Available online at https://papers.ssrn.com/sol3/papers.cfm?abstract_id=3233809.

Mohammadi, A., and Shafi, K. (2017, March). How wise are crowd? A comparative study of crowd and institutions in peer-to-business online lending markets. In *2017 Annual Meeting of the Academy of Management, AOM 2017*.

Mollick, E. (2014). The dynamics of crowdfunding: An exploratory study. *Journal of business venturing, 29*(1), 1–16.

Mollick, E., and Robb, A. (2016). Democratizing innovation and capital access: The role of crowdfunding. *California Management Review, 58*(2), 72–87.

Ordanini, A., Miceli, L., Pizzetti, M., and Parasuraman, A. (2011). Crowdfunding: Transforming customers into investors through innovative service platforms. *Journal of Service Management, 22*, 443–470.

Piva, E., and Rossi-Lamastra, C. (2018). Human capital signals and entrepreneurs' success in equity crowdfunding. *Small Business Economics, 51*, 667–686.

Ralcheva, A., and Roosenboom, P. (2019). *Forecasting success in equity crowdfunding*. Available at SSRN 3260140.

Shane, S., and Cable, D. (2002). Network ties, reputation, and the financing of new ventures. *Management Science, 48*(3), 364–381.

Sørensen, J. B., and Fassiotto, M. A. (2011). Organizations as fonts of entrepreneurship. *Organization Science, 22*(5), 1322–1331.

Stam, W., and Elfring, T. (2008). Entrepreneurial orientation and new venture performance: The moderating role of intra-and extraindustry social capital. *Academy of Management Journal, 51*(1), 97–111.

Vismara, S. (2016). Equity retention and social network theory in equity crowdfunding. *Small Business Economics, 46*, 579–590.

Vismara, S. (2018a). *Signaling to overcome inefficiencies in crowdfunding markets* (pp. 29–56). Springer International Publishing.

Vismara, S. (2018b). Information cascades among investors in equity crowdfunding. *Entrepreneurship Theory and Practice, 42*(3), 467–497.

Vulkan, N., Åstebro, T., and Sierra, M. F. (2016). Equity crowdfunding: A new phenomena. *Journal of Business Venturing Insights, 5*, 37–49.

Zhao, Y., Xie, X., and Yang, L. (2020), Female entrepreneurs and equity crowdfunding: The consequential roles of lead investors and venture stages. *International Entrepreneurship and Management Journal*, 1–29. https://doi.org/10.1007/s11365-020-00659-w

CHAPTER 5

Conclusions

Francesca Battaglia

Abstract This chapter draws conclusions on the topic addressed in the book. Since traditional funding channels, such as private equity, institutional capital, and bank financing, have exhibited biases against female entrepreneurs, it concludes that female entrepreneurs have to turn to crowdfunding, as an alternative funding channel. The chapter underlines that the book's findings hold important policy implications, urging regulators to facilitate the development of alternative finance and foster a level playing field across European countries.

Keywords Alternative funding channel · Equity crowdfunding · Female entrepreneurial development · Policy implications · Actions to combat gender disparities · Actions to promote inclusive financial landscape

Traditional funding channels such as private equity, institutional capital, and bank financing have exhibited biases against female entrepreneurs, leading to a minority representation of women in key fields. The presence of underrepresentation is clearly demonstrated by statistical data that indicates a notable disparity in the proportion of venture capital funding allocated to enterprises managed by women. The aforementioned disadvantages are not exclusive to the United States; they are also evident in

F. Battaglia and E. Giusi Gaeta, *Women in Alternative Finance*,
https://doi.org/10.1007/978-3-031-43467-9_5

Europe. In this region, women face several obstacles when it comes to obtaining financing, knowledge, business networks, and training.

To overcome these obstacles, the European Commission has been actively promoting and supporting female entrepreneurship through various initiatives. However, due to limited access to traditional venture capital, female entrepreneurs have turned to alternative funding channels such as crowdfunding. Early evidence suggests that women may not face the same disadvantages in crowdfunding as they do in traditional markets, and in fact, they may even outperform men in terms of campaign success rates.

By focusing on the equity crowdfunding context, this book contributes fresh evidence to the relationship between female entrepreneurship and alternative finance. The empirical analysis conducted in the Italian equity crowdfunding market between 2014 and 2020 reveals that equity crowdfunding can serve as an effective funding channel for female entrepreneurs, especially in countries where gender disparities in entrepreneurship are more pronounced. These findings have practical implications for start-ups and crowdfunding platforms, emphasising the importance of understanding the factors that investors perceive as quality signals to increase the likelihood of campaign success.

Moreover, the book's findings hold important policy implications, urging regulators to facilitate the development of alternative finance and foster a level playing field across European countries. With the increasing global sensitivity to gender inequality, international initiatives have been established to combat disparities and promote equal opportunities for women's growth. However, more concrete efforts are needed at the national level to address the barriers that hinder women's access to credit offered by banks, as this aspect has been relatively neglected. Policymakers have the power to drive change by implementing specific action plans and rules that support women in alternative finance, leading to more balanced economic growth and overall societal progress.

In summary, this book highlights the significance of equity crowdfunding as a conducive platform for the advancement of female entrepreneurship. It underscores the crucial involvement of policymakers in implementing effective measures to address gender inequalities and foster a financial environment that is more inclusive and equitable.

References

Agier, I., and Szafarz, A. (2013). Microfinance and gender: Is there a glass ceiling on loan size? *World Development*, *42*, 165–181.

Agrawal, A., Catalini, C., & Goldfarb, A. (2015). Crowdfunding: Geography, social networks, and the timing of investment decisions. *Journal of Economics & Management Strategy*, *24*(2), 253–274.

Ahl, H. (2006). Why research on women entrepreneurs needs new directions. *Entrepreneurship Theory and Practice*, *30*(5), 595–621.

Ahlers, G. K., Cumming, D., Günther, C., and Schweizer, D. (2015). Signaling in equity crowdfunding. *Entrepreneurship Theory and Practice*, *39*(4), 955–980.

Alesina, A. F., and Ardagna, S. (2013). The design of fiscal adjustments. *Tax Policy and the Economy*, *27*(1), 19–68.

Alesina, A. F., Lotti, F., and Mistrulli, P. E. (2013). Do women pay more for credit? Evidence from Italy. *Journal of the European Economic Association*, *11*(1), 45–66.

Allison, T. H., Davis, B. C., Short, J. C., and Webb, J. W. (2015). Crowdfunding in a prosocial microlending environment: Examining the role of intrinsic versus extrinsic cues. *Entrepreneurship Theory and Practice*, *39*(1), 53–73.

Andreoni, J. (1990). Impure altruism and donations to public goods: A theory of warm-glow giving. *The Economic Journal*, *100*(401), 464–477.

Angerer, M., Brem, A., Kraus, S., and Peter, A. (2017). Start-up funding via equity crowdfunding in Germany: A qualitative analysis of success factors. *The Journal of Entrepreneurial Finance*, *19*(1), 1–34.

F. Battaglia and E. Giusi Gaeta, *Women in Alternative Finance*, https://doi.org/10.1007/978-3-031-43467-9

Bapna, S., and Ganco, M. (2018). Gender gaps in equity crowdfunding: Evidence from a randomized field experiment. *Management Science, 7*, 1–32. https://doi.org/10.1287/mnsc.2020.3644.

Barbi, M., and Mattioli, S. (2019). Human capital, investor trust, and equity crowdfunding. *Research in International Business and Finance, 49*, 1–12.

Becker-Blease, J. R., and Sohl, J. E. (2007). Do women-owned businesses have equal access to angel capital? *Journal of Business Venturing*, *22*(4), 503–521.

Belleflamme, P., Lambert, T., and Schwienbacher, A. (2013). Individual crowdfunding practices. *Venture Capital*, *15*(4), 313–333.

Belleflamme, P., Lambert, T., and Schwienbacher, A. (2014). Crowdfunding: Tapping the right crowd. *Journal of Business Venturing*, *29*(5), 585–609.

Belt, B. D., Brummer, C., and Gorfine, D. (2012). *Crowdfunding: Maximizing the promise and minimizing the peril*. Washington, DC: Milken Institute.

Bigelow, C. A., Pereira, G. A., Warmsley, A., Cohen, J., Getrajdman, C., Moshier, E., and Stone, J. (2014a). Risk factors for new-onset late postpartum preeclampsia in women without a history of preeclampsia. *American Journal of Obstetrics and Gynecology*, *210*(4), 338-e1.

Bigelow, L., Lundmark, L., McLean Parks, J., and Wuebker, R. (2014b). Skirting the issues: Experimental evidence of gender bias in IPO prospectus evaluations. *Journal of Management*, *40*(6), 1732–1759.

Bird, B., and Brush, C. (2002). A gendered perspective on organizational creation. *Entrepreneurship Theory and Practice*, *26*(3), 41–65.

Block, J., Hornuf, L., and Moritz, A. (2018). Which updates during an equity crowdfunding campaign increase crowd participation? *Small Business Economics, 50*(1), 3–27.

Buttner, E. H., and Rosen, B. (1988). Bank loan officers' perceptions of the characteristics of men, women, and successful entrepreneurs. *Journal of Business Venturing*, *3*(3), 249–258.

Canning, J., Haque, M., and Wang, Y. (2012). *Women at the wheel: Do female executives drive start-up success*. Dow Jones and Company.

Canning, D., and Schultz, T. P. (2012). The economic consequences of reproductive health and family planning. *The Lancet*, *380*(9837), 165–171.

Carter, N. M., Gartner, W. B., Shaver, K. G., and Gatewood, E. J. (2003). The career reasons of nascent entrepreneurs. *Journal of Business Venturing*, *18*(1), 13–39.

Carter, S., and Rosa, P. (1998). Indigenous rural firms: Farm enterprises in the UK. *International Small Business Journal*, *16*(4), 15–27.

Ciuchta, M. P., Letwin, C., Stevenson, R. M., and McMahon, S. R. (2016). Regulatory focus and information cues in a crowdfunding context. *Applied Psychology*, *65*(3), 490–514.

Coleman S. (2000). Access to capital and terms of credit: A comparison of men– and women–owned small businesses. *Journal of Small Business Management, 38*(3), 37–52.

Coleman, M., and Bush, T. (2000). Leadership and strategic management in education. In *Leadership and strategic management in education* (pp. 1–96). Sage.

Coleman, S., and Robb, A. (2009), A comparison of new firm financing by gender: Evidence from the Kauffman Firm Survey data. *Small Business Economics, 33*, 397–411. https://doi.org/10.1007/s11187-009-9205-7.

Coleman, S., and Robb, A. (2016). Financing high growth women-owned enterprises: Evidence from the United States. In *Women's entrepreneurship in global and local contexts* (pp. 183–202). Edward Elgar Publishing.

Colombo, M. G., Franzoni, C., and Rossi–Lamastra, C. (2015). Internal social capital and the attraction of early contributions in crowdfunding. *Entrepreneurship Theory and Practice, 39*(1), 75–100.

Connell, R. W. (1990). An iron man: The body and some contradictions of hegemonic masculinity. In M. Messner, and D. Sabo (Eds.), *Sport, men and the gender order*. Champaign, IL: Human Kinetics Books.

Connell, R. W., and Messerschmidt, J. W. (2005). Hegemonic masculinity: Rethinking the concept. *Gender & Society, 19*(6), 829–859.

Constantinidis, C., Cornet, A., and Asandei, S. (2006). Financing of women-owned ventures: The impact of gender and other owner-and firm-related variables. *Venture Capital, 8*(02), 133–157.

Courtney, C., Dutta, S., and Li, Y. (2017). Resolving information asymmetry: Signaling, endorsement, and crowdfunding success. *Entrepreneurship Theory and Practice, 41*(2), 265–290.

Cumming, D. J., Leboeuf, G., and Schwienbacher, A. (2015). *Crowdfunding models: Keep-it-all vs*. Available at SSRN 2447567.

De Buysere, K., Gajda, O., Kleverlaan, R., Marom, D., and Klaes, M. (2012). A framework for European crowdfunding.

Du Rietz, A., and Henrekson, M. (2000). Testing the female underperformance hypothesis. *Small Business Economics, 14*, 1–10.

Eagly, A. H. (1987). *Sex differences in social behavior: A social-role interpretation.* Hillsdale, NJ: Lawrence Erlbaum.

Eagly, A. H., and Carli, L. L. (2003). The female leadership advantage: An evaluation of the evidence. *The Leadership Quarterly, 14*(6), 807–834.

Eagly, A. H., and Karau, S. J. (2002). Role congruity theory of prejudice toward female leaders. *Psychological review, 109*(3), 573.

Eagly, A. H., and Kite, M. E. (1987). Are stereotypes of nationalities applied to both women and men? *Journal of Personality and Social Psychology, 53*(3), 451.

Eckes, T. (2002). Paternalistic and envious gender stereotypes: Testing predictions from the stereotype content model. *Sex Roles*, *47*(3/4), 99.

Eddleston, K. A., Ladge, J. J., Mitteness, C., and Balachandra, L. (2016). Do you see what I see? Signaling effects of gender and firm characteristics on financing entrepreneurial ventures. *Entrepreneurship Theory and Practice*, *40*(3), 489–514.

Epstein, L. G., and Schneider, M. (2008). Ambiguity, information quality, and asset pricing. *The Journal of Finance*, *63*(1), 197–228.

Fabowale, L., Orser, B., and Riding, A. (1995). Gender, structural factors, and credit terms between Canadian small businesses and financial institutions. *Entrepreneurship Theory and Practice*, *19*(4), 41–65.

Fay, M., and Williams, L. (1993). Gender bias and the availability of business loans. *Journal of Business Venturing*, *8*(4), 363–376.

Fiske, S. T., and Taylor, S. E. (1991). *Social cognition*. McGraw-Hill Book Company.

Fiske, S. T., Cuddy, A. J., Glick, P., and Xu, J. (2002). A model of (often mixed) stereotype content: Competence and warmth respectively follow from perceived status and competition. *Journal of Personality and Social Psychology*, *82*(6), 878.

Freear, J., and Wetzel Jr, W. E. (1992). The informal venture capital market in the 1990s. In D. L. Sexton and J. D. Kasarda (Eds.), *State of the art of entrepreneurship* (pp. 462–486). Boston, MA: PWS-Kent.

Freear, J., Sohl, J. E., and Wetzel Jr, W. E. (1992). The investment attitudes, behavior and characteristics of high net worth individuals. *Frontiers of Entrepreneurship Research*, *16*, 374–387.

Gorbatai, A., and Nelson, L. (2015). *The narrative advantage: Gender and the language of crowdfunding*. Haas School of Business UC Berkeley. Research Papers, 1–32.

Greenberg, J., and Mollick, E. (2017). Activist choice homophily and the crowdfunding of female founders. *Administrative Science Quarterly*, *62*(2), 341–374.

Guenther, C., Johan, S., and Schweizer, D. (2018). Is the crowd sensitive to distance?—How investment decisions differ by investor type. *Small Business Economics*, *50*, 289–305.

Haines Jr, G. H., Orser, B. J., and Riding, A. L. (1999). Myths and realities: An empirical study of banks and the gender of small business clients. *Canadian Journal of Administrative Sciences/Revue Canadienne des Sciences de l'Administration*, *16*(4), 291–307.

Harrington, K. (2014, February 7). *Cashing in on crowdfunding*. Forbes, Entrepreneurs.

Harrington, K., Flint, A., and Healey, M. (2014). Engagement through partnership: Students as partners in learning and teaching in higher education.

Hertz, N. (2011). *Women and banks: Are female customers facing discrimination?* London: Institute for Public Policy Research. Available online at https://www.ippr.org/files/images/media/files/publication/2011/11/womenbanks_Nov2011_8186.pdf (last accessed: February 8, 2021).

Hemer, J. (2011). *A snapshot on crowdfunding* (No. R2/2011). Arbeitspapiere Unternehmen und Region.

Hinchliffe, E. (2019, January 30). In 2018, all female founders put together got $10 billion less than juul. *Fortune*. https://fortune.com/2019/01/28/funding-female-founders-2018/

Hisrich, R., and Brush, C. (1984). *The woman entrepreneur: Management skills and business problems*. University of Illinois at Urbana-Champaign's Academy for Entrepreneurial Leadership Historical Research Reference in Entrepreneurship.

Hoenig, D., and Henkel, J. (2015). Quality signals? The role of patents, alliances, and team experience in venture capital financing. *Research Policy, 44*(5), 1049–1064.

Hornuf, L., and Neuenkirch, M. (2016). Pricing shares in equity crowdfunding. *Research Papers in Economics*, (7/15).

Horvat, E. A., and Papamarkou, T. (2017, September). Gender differences in equity crowdfunding. In *Proceedings of the AAAI conference on human computation and crowdsourcing* (Vol. 5, pp. 51–60).

Ingram, C., and Teigland, R. (2013). *Crowdfunding among IT Entrepreneurs in Sweden*. Stockholm: Stockholm School of Economics.

International Finance Corporation (2021, December). *IFC Annual Report 2021*. World Bank Publications - Books, The World Bank Group, number 36334.

Johnson, M. A., Stevenson, R. M., and Letwin, C. R. (2018). A woman's place is in the… startup! Crowdfunder judgments, implicit bias, and the stereotype content model. *Journal of Business Venturing*, *33*(6), 813–831.

Kalleberg, A. L., and Leicht, K. T. (1991). Gender and organizational performance: Determinants of small business survival and success. *Academy of Management Journal*, *34*(1), 136–161.

Kunz, M. M., Englisch, O., Beck, J., & Bretschneider, U. (2016). Sometimes you win, sometimes you learn: Success factors in reward-based crowdfunding. *Multikonferenz Wirtschaftsinformatik (MKWI), Ilmenau, 2016*, 467–478.

Lebraty, J. F., and Lobre-Lebraty, K. (2013). *Crowdsourcing: One step beyond*. Wiley.

Lin, M., Prabhala, N. R., and Viswanathan, S. (2013). Judging borrowers by the company they keep: Friendship networks and information asymmetry in online peer-to-peer lending. *Management science, 59*(1), 17–35.

López-Zafra, E., Garcia-Retamero, R., and Eagly, A. H. (2009). Congruenza del ruolo di genere e aspirazioni delle donne a posizioni di leadership. *Giornale di psicologia sociale* , *24*(1), 99–108.

Lukkarinen, A., Teich, J. E., Wallenius, H., and Wallenius, J. (2016). Success drivers of online equity crowdfunding campaigns. *Decision Support Systems*, *87*, 26–38.

Malaga, R., Mamonov, S., and Rosenblum, J. (2018). Gender difference in equity crowdfunding: An exploratory analysis. *International Journal of Gender and Entrepreneurship, 10*(4), 332–343.

Marom, D., Robb, A., and Sade, O. (2014). *Gender dynamics in crowdfunding (kickstarter).* SSRN Working Paper, 2442954, 1–64.

Marom, D., Robb, A., and Sade, O. (2016). *Gender Dynamics in Crowdfunding (Kickstarter): Evidence on entrepreneurs, investors, deals and taste-based discrimination.* Investors, Deals and Taste-Based Discrimination.

Massolution, C. L. (2012). Crowdfunding industry report: Market trends, composition and crowdfunding platforms.

McGuire, E. (2020). Can equity crowdfunding close the gender gap in startup finance? Available online at https://papers.ssrn.com/sol3/papers.cfm?abstract_id=3233809.

McKechnie, S. A., Ennew, C. T., and Read, L. H. (1998). The nature of the banking relationship: A comparison of the experiences of male and female small business owner. *International Small Business Journal*, *16*(3), 39–55.

McKinsey & Company (2015). *The power of parity: How advancing women's equality can add $12 trillion to global growth*, September. Available at: https://www.mckinsey.com/featured-insights/employment-and-growth/how-advancing-womens-equality-can-add-12-trillion-to-global-growth.

Mohammadi, A., and Shafi, K. (2017, March). How wise are crowd? A comparative study of crowd and institutions in peer-to-business online lending markets. In *2017 Annual Meeting of the Academy of Management, AOM 2017.*

Mollick, E. (2014). The dynamics of crowdfunding: An exploratory study. *Journal of Business Venturing*, *29*(1), 1–16.

Mollick, E., and Robb, A. (2016). Democratizing innovation and capital access: The role of crowdfunding. *California Management Review*, *58*(2), 72–87.

Moss, T. W., Neubaum, D. O., and Meyskens, M. (2015). The effect of virtuous and entrepreneurial orientations on microfinance lending and repayment: A signaling theory perspective. *Entrepreneurship Theory and Practice, 39*(1), 27–52.

Muravyev, A., Talavera, O., and Schäfer, D. (2009). Entrepreneurs' gender and financial constraints: Evidence from international data. *Journal of Comparative Economics*, *37*(2), 270–286.

Neeley, L., and Van Auken, H. (2010). Differences between female and male entrepreneurs' use of bootstrap financing. *Journal of Developmental Entrepreneurship*, *15*(01), 19–34.

OECD (2016). *Entrepreneurship at a Glance*. Paris: OECD Publishing.

OECD (2018). *OECD toolkit for mainstreaming and implementing gender equality: Implementing the 2015 OECD recommendation on gender equality in public life*. https://www.oecd.org/gender/governance/toolkit/toolkit-for-mainstreaming-and-implementinggender-equality.pdf.

OECD (2021). *Development finance for gender equality and women's empowerment: A 2021 snapshot*. OECD DAC network on gender equality (gendernet). Available at: https://www.oecd.org/development/gender-development/Development-finance-for-gender-equality-2021.pdf.

OECD (2022a). *G7 dashboard on gender gaps – Germany*. Paris: OECD Publishing. https://www.g7germany.de/resource/blob/974430/2058072/5eafec9454770407b4f5719778ff7f50/2022-06-28-gender-gap-germany-data.pdf?download=1

OECD (2022b). *G7 dashboard on gender gaps – Italy*. Paris: OECD Publishing. https://www.g7germany.de/resource/blob/974430/2058170/3f90a9cb877a250f56245ede5adbf53a/2022-06-28-gender-gap-italy-data.pdf?download=1

OECD (2022c). *G7 dashboard on gender gaps – USA*. Paris: OECD Publishing. www.bmfsfj.de/resource/blob/199066/66728e8bae6287b5e8b2848d41fe53a6/g7-dashboard-on-gender-gaps-usa-data.pdf.

OECD (2023). *Joining forces for gender equality: What is holding us back?* Paris: OECD Publishing.

Ongena, S., and Popov, A. (2015). *Gender Bias and Credit Access*. ECB Working Paper Series, no. 1822, July 2015.

Ordanini, A., Miceli, L., Pizzetti, M., and Parasuraman, A. (2011). Crowdfunding: Transforming customers into investors through innovative service platforms. *Journal of Service Management*, *22*, 443–470.

Ozmel, U., Reuer, J. J., and Gulati, R. (2013). Signals across multiple networks: How venture capital and alliance networks affect interorganizational collaboration. *Academy of Management Journal*, *56*(3), 852–866.

Petty, J. S., and Gruber, M. (2011). "In pursuit of the real deal": A longitudinal study of VC decision making. *Journal of Business Venturing*, *26*(2), 172–188.

Piva, E., and Rossi-Lamastra, C. (2018). Human capital signals and entrepreneurs' success in equity crowdfunding. *Small Business Economics*, *51*, 667–686.

Popov, A. A., and Rocholl, J. (2015). Financing constraints, employment, and labor compensation: Evidence from the subprime mortgage crisis.

Prasad, P., and Prasad, A. (2000). Stretching the iron cage: The constitution and implications of routine workplace resistance. *Organization Science*, *11*(4), 387–403.

Prasad, D., Bruton, G. D., and Vozikis, G. (2000). Signaling value to business angels: The proportion of the entrepreneur's net worth invested in a new venture as a decision signal. *Venture Capital: An International Journal of Entrepreneurial Finance, 2*(3), 167–182.

Ralcheva, A., and Roosenboom, P. (2019). *Forecasting success in equity crowdfunding*. Available at SSRN 3260140.

Ralcheva, A., and Roosenboom, P. (2020). Forecasting success in equity crowdfunding. *Small Business Economics*, *55*, 39–56.

Rosa, P., and Hamilton, D. (1994). Gender and ownership in UK small firms. *Entrepreneurship Theory and Practice*, *18*(3), 11–27.

Rosa, P., Carter, S., and Hamilton, D. (1996). Gender as a determinant of small business performance: Insights from a British study. *Small Business Economics, 8*(6), 463–478. http://www.jstor.org/stable/40228670.

Rubinton, B. J. (2011). Crowdfunding: Disintermediated investment banking. Available at SSRN 1807204.

Schein, V. E., and Davidson, M. J. (1993). Think Manager, Think Male. *Management Development Review*, *6*(3). https://doi.org/10.1108/EUM0000000000738.

Shane, S., and Cable, D. (2002). Network ties, reputation, and the financing of new ventures. *Management Science*, *48*(3), 364–381.

Sørensen, J. B., and Fassiotto, M. A. (2011). Organizations as fonts of entrepreneurship. *Organization Science*, *22*(5), 1322–1331.

Spence, M. (1973, August). Job market signaling. *The Quarterly Journal of Economics, 87*(3), 355–374. https://doi.org/10.2307/1882010.

Spence, J. T., Helmreich, R., and Stapp, J. (1973). A short version of the Attitudes toward Women Scale (AWS). *Bulletin of the Psychonomic Society*, *2*(4), 219–220.

Stam, W., and Elfring, T. (2008). Entrepreneurial orientation and new venture performance: The moderating role of intra-and extraindustry social capital. *Academy of Management Journal*, *51*(1), 97–111.

Steinberg, M. (2012). *Anime's media mix: Franchising toys and characters in Japan*. University of Minnesota Press.

Tosi, H. L., and Einbender, S. W. (1985). The effects of the type and amount of information in sex discrimination research: A meta-analysis. *Academy of Management Journal*, *28*(3), 712–723.

UN Women (2017). *Annual report 2016–2017*. Available at: annualreport.unwomen.org

Vismara, S. (2016). Equity retention and social network theory in equity crowdfunding. *Small Business Economics*, *46*, 579–590.

Vismara, S. (2018a). *Signaling to overcome inefficiencies in crowdfunding markets* (pp. 29–56). Springer International Publishing.

Vismara, S. (2018b). Information cascades among investors in equity crowdfunding. *Entrepreneurship Theory and Practice, 42*(3), 467–497.

Vulkan, N., Åstebro, T., and Sierra, M. F. (2016). Equity crowdfunding: A new phenomena. *Journal of Business Venturing Insights, 5*, 37–49.

Wicks, M. (2013). *Crowdfunding-an introduction.* Victoria: Blue Beetle Books.

Zhao, L., and Shneor, R. (2020). Donation crowdfunding: Principles and donor behaviour. In *Advances in crowdfunding: Research and practice* (pp. 145–160). Springer.

Zhao, Y., Xie, X., and Yang, L. (2020), Female entrepreneurs and equity crowdfunding: The consequential roles of lead investors and venture stages. *International Entrepreneurship and Management Journal*, 1–29. https://doi.org/10.1007/s11365-020-00659-w

Index

F. Battaglia and E. Giusi Gaeta, *Women in Alternative Finance*,
https://doi.org/10.1007/978-3-031-43467-9

U

V

The manufacturer's authorised representative in the EU is Springer Nature Customer Service Centre GmbH, Europaplatz 3, 69115 Heidelberg, Germany. If you have any concerns regarding our products, please contact ProductSafety@springernature.com

Printed and bound by CPI Group (UK) Ltd, Croydon, CR0 4YY
01/10/2026
02225879-0002